THE
LEADERSHIP TRAINING ACTIVITY BOOK

50 Exercises for Building Effective Leaders

LOIS B. HART, Ed.D.
CHARLOTTE S. WAISMAN, Ph.D.

AMACOM
AMERICAN MANAGEMENT ASSOCIATION
New York | Atlanta | Brussels
Chicago | Mexico City | San Francisco
Shanghai | Tokyo | Toronto | Washington, D. C.

Special discounts on bulk quantities of AMACOM books are available to corporations, professional associations, and other organizations. For details, contact Special Sales Department, AMACOM, a division of American Management Association, 1601 Broadway, New York, NY 10019.
Tel: 800-250-5308. Fax: 518-891-2372.
E-mail: specialsls@amanet.org
Website: www.amacombooks.org/go/specialsales
To view all AMACOM titles go to: www.amacombooks.org

Library of Congress Cataloging-in-Publication Data

Hart, Lois Borland.
    The leadership training activity book / Lois B. Hart, Charlotte S. Waisman ; foreword by James M. Kouzes.
        p.   cm.
    Includes index.
    ISBN-13: 978-0-8144-7262-0
    ISBN-10: 0-8144-7262-1
    1. Leadership—Study and teaching—Activity programs.   I. Waisman, Charlotte S.   II. Title.
HD57.7.H383   2005
658.4'092—dc22

                                                                 2004019036

Printing number

10   9   8   7

CONTENTS

PART ONE
Lay the Groundwork, Energize Participants, and Then Close 1

LIST OF HANDOUTS AND JOB AIDS

Templates of the handouts and job aids listed below are available in pdf format for you to download at www.amacombooks.org/leadershipact.

FOREWORD

There's a scene in the film adaptation of Muriel Spark's classic, *The Prime of Miss Jean Brodie,* during which Head Mistress McKay calls Miss Brodie to her office to chastise Miss Brodie for her somewhat unorthodox teaching methods.[1] Head Mistress McKay comments on the precocity of Miss Brodie's students. Miss Brodie accepts this as a compliment, not a criticism and says:

"To me education is a leading out. The word education comes from the root 'ex,' meaning 'out,' and 'duco,' 'I lead.' To me education is simply a leading out of what is already there."

To this head mistress McKay responds rather haughtily, saying, "I had hoped there might also be a certain amount of putting in."

Miss Brodie laughs at this notion and replies, "That would not be education, but intrusion."

Lois Hart and Charlotte Waisman would make Jean Brodie proud. *50 Activities for Developing Leaders* is not about "putting in." It's about leading out of what is already in the hearts and minds of learners. That's as it should be, for development should never be intrusive. It should never be about filling someone full of facts or skills. It just won't work. Education should always be liberating. It should be about releasing what is already inside us.

Leadership development is self-development. The quest for leadership is first an inner quest to discover who you are. That is clearly the premise of this wonderful collection of developmental activities. They guide learners on that fascinating journey of self-awareness and self-confidence that can only come from experiencing something *in* themselves *for* themselves. Learning to lead is about discovering what *you* value. About what inspires *you*. About what challenges *you*. About what gives *you* power and

Portions of this foreword are adapted from *The Leadership Challenge* by James M. Kouzes and Barry Z. Posner. San Francisco: Jossey-Bass, 2002. Copyright © 2003 James M. Kouzes and Barry Z. Posner. All rights reserved.

[1] This scene is from the film version of *The Prime of Miss Jean Brodie,* produced by Robert Fryer and directed by Robert Neame. Screenplay by Jay Presson Allen. Twentieth Century Fox Productions, 1968. Adapted from the novel, *The Prime of Miss Jean Brodie,* by Muriel Spark (New York: Perennial Classics, 1999).

competence. About what encourages *you*. When you discover these things about your-self, you'll know what it takes to lead those qualities out of others. I assure you that if you engage others in the experiences in this volume, that's exactly what will happen.

Sometimes liberation is as uncomfortable as intrusion, but in the end when you discover it for yourself you know that what's inside is what you found there and what belongs there. It's not something put inside you by someone else; you discover you've had the gifts all along.

But just when you think that it's the experience that's the teacher, you quickly learn that it's really not what this is all about. Experiential learning *is* essential to mas-tery, but there's another critical lesson awaiting you and your learners.

In the process of my own development as an adult educator, I was extremely for-tunate to have participated in programs led by some of the most seasoned training professionals in the business. One of them was Fred Margolis. Fred was a student of Malcolm Knowles, the father of the theory and method of adult learning known as andragogy. Fred was a master, and he taught me a lesson in the early 1970's that has shaped everything I've done as an educator since then.

I was doing some work in Washington, D. C., and after a day of training Fred and I met at an Italian restaurant for dinner. During our dinner, Fred asked me, "Jim, what's the best way to learn something?" Since I'd been extensively involved in experiential learning, I confidently told Fred the obvious: "The best way to learn something is to experience it yourself."

"No," Fred responded. "The *best* way to learn something is to *teach* it to somebody else!" Boing! That was one of those moments when your brain does a double take, and you realize that you've just heard something extremely profound and a whole new world is about to unfold.

What I learned that day from Fred—and I continue to learn every day I am with a group—is that the act of teaching is an act of learning. The deepest kind of learning. You've probably felt the impact of this yourself—whether you're an expert or a novice. The moment you're asked to teach you start to think, study, worry, and prepare. In the process you become consumed by learning. You know you're on the line. You're going to have to perform live in front of others, and you better know your stuff. You've got to learn at a deeper level.

That lesson—*we learn best when we teach someone else*—has shaped my style more profoundly than any other lesson on learning. It inspires me daily to find new ways for people to teach each other. When participants put themselves out there as role models or subject matter experts, I know and they know that they've got to reach in-side a lot deeper than if I just ask them to take part in a simulation.

This is the most important benefit of Lois and Charlotte's contribution. They don't just ask people to be learners. They ask participants to be teachers. It's the teaching that participants do *after* the experience that is the most critical part of the process.

That's when everyone knows they've internalized it, made it a part of themselves. And when you've internalized it, you can externalize it; you can teach it to others.

All of this is reinforced by something else that my coauthor Barry Posner and I found in doing research for the third edition of *The Leadership Challenge.* What we uncovered is that the best leaders are the best learners. And what would you say comes first, the capacity to learn or the capacity to lead? We think that learning comes first. Learning to lead comes second. So what you are doing by fully engaging others in the *experience* of learning—not just the experience of leading—will benefit them in every other aspect of their lives. That is the magic and the joy of leading out what is already there!

Jim Kouzes
San Jose, California
April 2003

PREFACE

As you pick up this book for the first time, I'm sure you're wondering how this book can help those who grapple with perhaps the most elusive type of training—leadership training?

Lois Hart founded the Women's Leadership Institute nearly six years ago. She began working regularly with Charlotte Waisman, a long-time friend and professional colleague, and soon came to appreciate Charlotte's talents as a coach, trainer, and mentor. Lois suggested that they write this book together because she believed that our collaborative efforts and diverse professional experiences will help other trainers.

We first needed to decide what leadership topics we would include. Long before the book you are now reading was ever in our consciousness, we as professionals were constantly searching for the best thinking on leadership theory. We continuously review what researchers and authors describe about leader competencies, skills, and attitudes; we read the major leadership books and theorists, and we discuss the goods and bads of each approach. As you will see in this book, we fully agree on one common approach.

We believe that Leadership itself is a critical competency, and we believe it can be taught. We suggest that leadership is a huge subject encompassing discrete actions and activities that can themselves be identified as competencies. It is hard to imagine a successful leader not having a very demonstrable capability and capacity for risk and risk-taking. So, Risk became one of the 50 topics!

After countless hours of study and discussion, we concluded that Jim Kouzes and Barry Posner have done the best research on leadership, which they describe in their book, *The Leadership Challenge*. Their original research for the *Leadership Practices Inventory* was with 120 MBA students (average age 29; 60% male). The current version of the book was based on surveys of 1,567 U.S. executives participating in public and private sector management-development seminars (12% of the participants were female). A separate survey collected information from managers in Australia, England, Germany, and the Netherlands.

Kouzes and Posner compared responses from 73 senior human resource management professionals (49 men and 24 women) attending the same conference. The women did not differ measurably in their responses from the men, with one exception: their self-reports on "Encouraging the Heart" showed higher ratings.

The researchers found no significant differences between a group of 137 federal government executives and a group of 197 private-sector executives; no significant differences between a group of 95 Australian managers and a group of 70 American mid-level managers; and no significant differences between a group of 170 European managers (English, German, and Dutch) and a group of 270 American managers.

Kouzes and Posner are continuing to systematically research the subject, conducting personal interviews and case studies with over 1,000 managers, as well as empirical investigations involving more than 45,000 participants. For more detailed information on their research, you can access their psychometric report and summaries of 150 doctoral dissertations on their Web site at www.leadershipchallenge.com.

When Lois authored *50 Activities for Developing Leaders* (HRD Press) in 1994, she recognized Kouzes and Posner's enormous contribution to the body of knowledge that forms the basis of the study of Leadership. Many other theories have been published since that time, but we have chosen to continue to build on Kouzes and Posner's work. We use their book *The Leadership Challenge* (now in its third edition) as the basis for the Women's Leadership Institute, a yearlong leadership development program now in its fifth year of implementation. A discussion of the topics that Kouzes and Posner pose is central to the work we do in our eleven full-day workshops. Having drawn on it for more than eight years, it was natural, as we thought about this book, to once again try to organize our thinking around their ideas.

We encourage you to read their work and see how our leadership activities play out as a demonstration of their model. Kouzes and Posner divide leadership competency into "five characteristics" of exemplary leadership—each covering behaviors that demonstrate personal leadership. "Inspire a Shared Vision" is one of these five "practices" and we are not surprised. Kouzes and Posner's work itself is so inspiring, we will direct your attention to it again and again as you read ours. We are honored to build from their base.

Field marketing reports clearly show that the teaching of Leadership is a continued, high-value endeavor. Trainers, teachers, and consultants, internal and external, are looking for current and updated sources of materials and curricula that are timely, interesting, and engaging to adult learners in business settings. The activities must be based on principles of adult learning and principles of accelerated learning, and must translate into value-added ways for the learner to produce business results. The better-cheaper-faster competitiveness of American business is still driving learning! The activities in our book are flexible and can be used in a variety of situations. We encourage you to select and modify our work so you can achieve any number of different outcomes that suit your particular circumstances.

At the first planning meeting for this book, Lois told Charlotte that she believes co-authoring is a dynamic way to write—that the process of bouncing ideas off one another is truly beneficial. Lois thoroughly enjoys sharing the creative process, and likes the challenge of being challenged. (Kouzes and Posner call the second tenet of Leadership "Challenge the Process.")

The ideas and activities in this book will help you and your colleagues. The ideas within it have been tested in many Leadership training situations. Each activity has been thoroughly test-driven and honed for its essential message. The first Kouzes-Posner tenet is "Model the Way," and many, many colleagues have generously shared their ideas with us. Their experiences have enriched this work, and we appreciate their contributions.

Finally, we thank Bob Carkhuff, our publisher. Thanks also to everyone at AMACOM Books and at Chernow Editorial Services, Inc. Also, if you adapt our materials to reflect your own special expertise, write us, call us, or e-mail us to share what you have done. We promise to pass it on! (The fourth Kouzes-Posner tenet is "Enable Others to Act.")

Enjoy our work; we truly enjoyed the process of bringing it to fruition.

Charlotte S. Waisman, Ph.D.
jottin1303@aol.com

Lois B. Hart, Ed.D.
lhart@seqnet.net
Denver, Colorado
2003

HOW TO GET THE MOST OUT OF THIS BOOK

We have strived to provide flexibility and options throughout the book, as well as explain how we have personally used each module. We are confident that you will be able to take our materials and modify them to meet your specific needs.

The current trend in training is to avoid daylong programs and, instead, offer one to three modules of one, two, or three hours each. If shorter sessions work best for you, consider choosing modules that can make up a longer Leadership program, but offer them in smaller chunks.

Most activities in this book come with an estimated time. Feel free to adapt that time frame as you see fit. Within some modules, we note that a particular section took us 5 minutes or 10 minutes; we hope these comments help you see that a simple question can lead to extensive group discussion. Again, your own situation will be the best guide.

We have also tried to supply you with an optimal group size. We often suggest twenty as an upper limit because one facilitator for 20 participants, in our opinion, is the best size for interaction and participation—and we certainly want each session to have those lively qualities! That said, if your group is 30, perhaps you can get a colleague to help you. You will know what is best for your training mode and comfort level.

Templates of all the handouts and job aids presented in this book will be available in pdf format for you to download from AMACOM's Web site. The address is www.amacombooks.org/leadershipact.

We have written this book as a get-up-and-do guide. We are not offering you lists of other books to read and other places to get ideas, unless they directly relate to the materials we have provided. Our delight would be e-mails, calls, and letters from each reader, to tell us of the many ways that you were able to adapt and re-structure our ideas. Play with your thoughts, build on our ideas, and make each training module truly your own.

ABOUT THE AUTHORS

Lois B. Hart, Ed.D., is the founder and Executive Director of the Women's Leadership Institute, a unique, yearlong program of mentoring, coaching and training executive women.

During the past thirty years, as President of Leadership Dynamics, she offered workshops, facilitation, organizational consulting and professional books to businesses, government agencies and non-profits throughout the United States.

Dr. Hart earned a BS from the University of Rochester, a MS from Syracuse University and her Ed.D. from the University of Massachusetts where she studied organizational behavior and leadership development with Dr. Kenneth Blanchard.

Lois has written 22 books and tapes including *50 Activities for Developing Leaders Vol. I, Faultless Facilitation-A Resource Guide and Instructor's Manual, Learning From Conflict* trainer's manual and the *Manager's Pocket Guide to Dealing with Conflict.* Other books include *Training Methods That Work, A Conference and Workshop Planner's Manual, Connections: Five Contact Points with Participants, Moving Up! Women, The Sexes at Work-Improving Work Relationships Between Men and Women* with Dr. David Dalke.

In 2002, Lois was named the Colorado Women's Leader of Excellence for her work with the Colorado Women's Leadership Coalition. Other recent honors include a lifetime membership from The American Society of Training and Development-Rocky Mt. Chapter who gave Lois this gift for her numerous contributions to the association.

Contact Lois at lhart@seqnet.net.

Charlotte S. Waisman, Ph.D., is a coach, trainer and team leader with The Women's Leadership Institute.

Diverse clients in corporations, small businesses, government, non-profits and universities have utilized her training, coaching, presentations and human resources' knowledge and experience. She has expertise in developing Mentoring programs, certifications in diagnostic tools such as the Myers Briggs Type Inventory and is also a Certified Behavioral Interviewer.

Her extensive work history includes human resources and training positions in a number of firms. Currently, Charlotte is the Director of Human Resources at Ischemia Technologies (a Denver biomedical research firm). In addition to those duties traditional for an HR Director, she also is in charge of the training program for ISO 9001 certification. Earlier, while at Keane, Inc., she was in charge of employee career development and planned the initiatives to prepare the staff for future positions of greater responsibility within the firm.

At Telectronics, a worldwide manufacturer/distributor of implantable arrhythmia control systems (i.e. Pacemakers and Defibrillators), she was responsible for the creation of a world class education and training program including succession planning and extensive career development.

Dr. Charlotte S. Waisman has a B.S., M.A., and Ph.D. from the School of Communication at Northwestern University in Evanston, Illinois. Her background also includes 14 years as a tenured professor of speech and communication at the University of Utah and Northeastern Illinois University.

Contact Charlotte at jottin1303@aol.com

ACKNOWLEDGMENTS
TO THE CONTRIBUTORS

Our book was made possible through the inspiration and contributions of many of our fine colleagues.

Jim Kouzes and Barry Posner, authors of *The Leadership Challenge, Encouraging the Heart and Credibility*, provided the well researched leadership model we describe in Activity 18: *The Leadership Challenge: The Kouzes-Posner Leadership Model*. We utilize their model, books and instruments throughout our Women's Leadership Institute program so our book's content was extensively influenced by their work. Jim Kouzes graciously wrote the Forward for which we are most appreciative.

Lois first learned about leadership while a graduate student with Ken Blanchard. Activity 32: *Flex Your Style*, was inspired from Ken's work on leadership style.

Ken, Lois and Mario Tamoyo created the model found in Activity 50: *Add Heart to Your Celebrations at Work*.

Activity 23: *Values—The Basis of Ethics*, and Activity 24: *Just Do the Right Thing: How to Make Ethical Decisions* were adapted from Dr. David D. Dalke and Sheryl Ankerstar's book, *Balancing Personal and Professional Ethics*.

Linda Rydberg, Nancy Whitsel, Brice Davis, and Joan French's experience inspired Activity 15: *Let's Meet! Form A Professional Resource Group*.

Activity 31: *Making Connections—Networking*, was adapted from the comprehensive work of Anne Baber and Lynne Waymon, authors of *Make Your Contacts Count*.

Every member of our Women's Leadership Institute's Leadership Team offered original creations for this volume. Our unique program and this book were truly the joint efforts of Linda Rydberg, Marilyn Laverty, Linda Bedinger and of course Lois and Charlotte.

Linda Rydberg's contributions include Activity 38: *Presenting with Pizzazz*, Activity 42: *Listen Up! The Leader as Coach*, Activity 43: *Pass It On! The Leader as Teacher*, and Activity 46: *Searching for Creativity*.

Linda Bedinger created Activity 37: *Toot Your Horn! Sell Yourself and Your Ideas*.

Marilyn Laverty contributed Activity 24, Dear *Diary* and collaborated with Charlotte on Activity 48, *Leadership Stations* and Activity 28 *Balancing Balls and Balancing Life.*

We sincerely thank each of these colleagues who, like us, are committed to the development of leaders.

Lois Hart
Charlotte Waisman

PART ONE

Lay the Groundwork, Energize Participants, and Then Close

Professional trainers always design workshops that will make such an impact on participants that they will retain and apply what was learned. The activities in Part One provide a variety of methods for laying the groundwork for the workshop, reenergizing participants as they learn, and allowing them to close the program on a meaningful note.

The activity *Get Them Ready* prepares participants for the upcoming workshop. Other activities are geared to work groups or teams that can work together on assignments. Some leadership skills, such as story-telling, can be introduced at the beginning of the workshop and then built on at later points. Journaling is another useful training technique; it gives participants an opportunity to reflect on what they have learned and then record their ideas for putting the learning into action. Leadership is also about passing on what we know; *The Exhibit Hall* is one way to encourage participants to share their wealth of knowledge and experience.

Most day-long workshops run out of energy about halfway through, mainly because people need to get up and move around. *Walk and Talk* reenergizes participants as they continue their exploration of leadership. Make the review fun with the *Koosh Ball Game* midway through or at the end of your program. Other closure activities focus on identifying what participants learned or wish to put into action: try the fun game called *Word Scrabble,* do some journaling with *Dear Diary,* and be sure to check out the complete description of how to form a Professional Resource Group.

GET THEM READY!
Pre-Workshop Meeting to Select and Prepare Your Participants in Advance

Overview of Activity

A straightforward explanation of how to plan and conduct a meeting to identify the leaders who will ultimately be part of your Leadership Training Group.

Objectives

→ To review participants' prior experiences with leadership development.
→ To identify participants' commitment to learning.
→ To identify participants' strengths and skills.
→ To identify the skills each participant needs to develop.
→ To fine-tune the future workshop design.

Setting Up the Activity

GROUP SIZE
Flexible

ESTIMATED TIME
30 to 40 minutes

TRAINING METHODS
→ Presentation
→ Structured warm-up activity

MATERIALS
None

EQUIPMENT AND SUPPLIES
None

ROOM SET-UP
Arrange chairs in a circle.

Comments

Your first connection with the participants is crucial, because it sets the tone for the workshop and provides you with an opportunity to outline the scope of the program. The fact that you took the time to carefully select and then contact participants beforehand indicates that you are taking their learning seriously.

The outcome of the workshop will depend on who the participants are, so think about the kinds of people who are likely to contribute the most. Who will benefit most from the experience? The following characteristics are often used to select participants for longer leadership-training programs:

→ Individuals who have expressed an interest in leadership.

→ Individuals who have time or who will take the time to learn the skills and then use them.

→ Individuals who are confident of their own abilities as managers and leaders.

→ Individuals who have the support of their managers to attend the program.

→ Individuals who demonstrate an interest in learning and in professional development.

Once you have selected the participants, use this activity before you begin the workshop. It will help focus participants on their expectations and needs. This activity will also assist them to identify what they already know and give you an opportunity to explain how the activity is organized.

No training can be successful without support from the organization's supervisors, managers, and executives. It is wise to involve managers in the section process but be sure that you provide the criteria.

Variation

One alternative to hand-picking participants is to select a random sample of individuals for this first meeting. Select both individuals who are likely to be supportive and interested in attending, as well as individuals who are skeptical. In your initial meeting, outline the goals of the program and ask them to tell you what they hope to get out of the workshop. We have found that participants who have been preselected often become promoters of the program. You may choose to communicate directly with the participants via E-mail.

Trainer's Notes for Activity 1

ADVANCE PREPARATION

➜ Develop your workshop plan, based on the information you already have about the organization and the individuals who will be participating.

➜ Draft and send out a letter to participants that explains the purpose of the workshop and provides details about the workshop meeting (time, location, purpose of workshop, and so forth).

STEP-BY-STEP PROCEDURE

Step 1: Introduce yourself and outline your qualifications as a leadership expert.

Step 2: Explain the goals of the workshop.

Step 3: Ask participants to share what they hope or need to get out of the workshop.

Step 4: Select a short activity that will give people an idea of what the typical workshop will be like (perhaps one of the warm-up activities found in this chapter, such as "Leadership Shield" or "Make It Rhyme with Leader"). For example, "Leadership Shield," with its active art project component, has been found to be a great activity for mixed gender groups.

Step 5: Explain the workshop arrangements: directions to the site, beginning and ending times, appropriate attire, refreshments, how you will handle interruptions (beepers, messages), and so on.

Step 6: Explain the benefits of attending the workshop, including how the organization as a whole benefits.

POST-ACTIVITY REVIEW

Take time shortly after conducting this activity to reflect on how it went, how engaged the participants were, and what questions they raised. Then, make notes that include how much time you actually spent on the activity.

2

GET THE IDEA?
Form *IDEA* Teams

Overview of Activity

Small groups that can process the large concepts presented in the Leadership Training area are a valuable way for participants to practice through exercises. "IDEA" stands for Innovation, Development, Enthusiasm, and Application—all ways that the participants can build their teams.

Objective

To introduce the IDEA team concept and explain how it will be used during the workshop.

Setting Up the Activity

GROUP SIZE
Up to 20 participants

ESTIMATED TIME
30 minutes to 1 hour

TRAINING METHODS
➔ Discussion
➔ Art project

MATERIALS
A large sign that reads "IDEA"

EQUIPMENT AND SUPPLIES
These will vary, depending on which team building activity you select.

ROOM SET-UP
Any seating arrangement is acceptable.

Comments

If your leadership program extends over several days or is conducted in two or more sessions, create small groups of 5 to 7 people who will meet periodically throughout the program's duration to work on a problem or case study, debrief the module, and generally lend support to one another. The small groups can remain together and form a Professional Resource Group, as suggested in Activity 14.

Trainer's Notes for Activity 2

ADVANCE PREPARATION

Decide how you will form the IDEA teams. Either set up heterogeneous groups in advance, or let the participants decide when you start the activity who will be in which group. If the participants know one another well, and it is important for people to work with those from the same department, then it would be best to let them choose their own group. If the participants don't know one another, it would be helpful for the trainers to make up the groupings in advance.

STEP-BY-STEP PROCEDURE

Step 1: Provide an overview of the purpose and use of IDEA teams in your program.

➔ The IDEA groups will give participants an opportunity to discuss issues, complete assignments, and share program experiences in smaller groups.

➔ The IDEA teams will act as support groups for participants throughout the program.

Step 2: Explain how the name IDEA was derived, using the large sign. Discuss what each letter means as you talk about the importance of the following four words and how they relate to your workshop:

I = Innovation

Leaders recognize the need for change and continuous improvement so they can lead others in creating innovations. In this workshop, you will experience some innovative and creative learning methods.

D = Development

Leaders encourage and provide resources for their followers' development and their own. In this workshop, you are experiencing professional development first hand.

E = Enthusiasm

Leaders need to display enthusiasm and a positive attitude, even during challenging times. In this workshop, we will create a positive environment to enhance your interpersonal relationships and accelerate your learning.

A = Application

Learning is incomplete without the opportunity to apply what has been learned. In this workshop, you will have the opportunity to apply what is presented.

Step 3: Organize participants into teams and immediately assign a team-building exercise or a task. Have participants meet in their IDEA teams once each day to complete tasks within selected modules.

Step 4: The IDEA groups you have just joined will give you an opportunity to discuss issues, complete assignments together, and share program experiences periodically. Your IDEA teams will also provide any additional support throughout the program. Additionally, use these groups to discuss workplace issues that may arise.

POST-ACTIVITY REVIEW

Take time shortly after conducting this activity to reflect on how it went, how engaged the participants were, and what questions they raised. Then, make notes that include how much time you actually spent on the activity.

3

LEADERSHIP SHIELD

Overview of Activity

Through participation in an art project, leaders identify their basic values and share them with others, so that participants who will be working together on assignments have a greater understanding of each other's strengths.

Objective

To have participants share some information about their backgrounds, values, philosophies of life, and leadership experiences.

Setting Up the Activity

GROUP SIZE
Up to 20 participants

ESTIMATED TIME
30 minutes

TRAINING METHODS
➜ Art project
➜ Reflection
➜ Discussion

MATERIALS
- → Handout 3.1: *Leadership Shield*
- → Sample family coat of arms/crest or shield, if possible

EQUIPMENT AND SUPPLIES
- → Several sets of colored markers for participants to share

- → Flipchart paper

- → One large poster with an outline of a shield, with one of the four following words in each section: background, philosophy of life, values, and leadership.

ROOM SET-UP
- → Move furniture away from the walls to create space for participants to hang up and stand next to large pieces of paper during the discussion.

- → Post the large poster as you prepare to open the activity.

Comments

Use this activity when you have sufficient space on the walls to post the shields. An alternative is to have participants complete their shields on copy paper. This is a popular activity; participants are able to work with categories of information that are interesting to them.

Trainer's Notes for Activity 3

STEP-BY-STEP PROCEDURE

Step 1: Ask which participants have a family coat of arms, crest, or shield. Ask those who respond positively to describe or draw a picture of it. Explain that the purpose is to develop a new symbol that emphasizes leadership.

Step 2: Distribute one sheet of flipchart paper and several colored markers to each participant. Ask participants to draw the outline of a crest or shield on the paper. Demonstrate by drawing the outline of a shield on your flipchart (or distribute Handout 3.1). As noted on the handout, a shield is a pictorial representation that may show one's values, beliefs, and ideas.

Step 3: Explain that four categories of information have been selected for representation on the shield or coat of arms. Announce one category at a time, and remind participants to leave space on their shield for all four. Allow them approximately two minutes to draw each response.

The categories, each of which should be represented in one quadrant of the shield are:

a. Two of your leadership skills.
b. The part of your current work that you like best.
c. Two values that influence how you lead others.
d. A recent success or accomplishment.

Step 4: Ask the participants to complete their coats of arms by writing their family names on the shield and adding a personal motto that they try to exemplify. If they wish, they can embellish their shields with other graphics or designs.

Step 5: Ask participants to explain what they have included on their shield, and why. Allow approximately one minute per person. (Participants might only have time to explain one part of it.)

Step 6: Briefly discuss how our backgrounds, values, and personal philosophies affect the ways we interact and lead. Tie what is shared by the participants into the content of your leadership program.

Step 7: Pose these questions:

1. Which quadrant was the easiest to complete, and why?

2. Which quadrant, if any, reveals something about you that others might not know?

3. Which quadrant demonstrates the values of your company?

VARIATIONS

→ Take a picture of each participant and affix it to each person's shield.

→ If you have more than 20 people or you need to save time, form groups of 5 to 6 participants for Step 5.

POST-ACTIVITY REVIEW

Take time shortly after conducting this activity to reflect on how it went, how engaged the participants were, and what questions they raised. Then, make notes that include how much time you actually spent on the activity.

Leadership Shield

Two of my leadership skills are my vision and creativity

What I like best about my work is the opportunity to influence others

Two of my values are my inclusiveness and integrity

One of my recent successes was to reorganize my department and save one-half FTE.

LEADERSHIP SHIELD (continued)

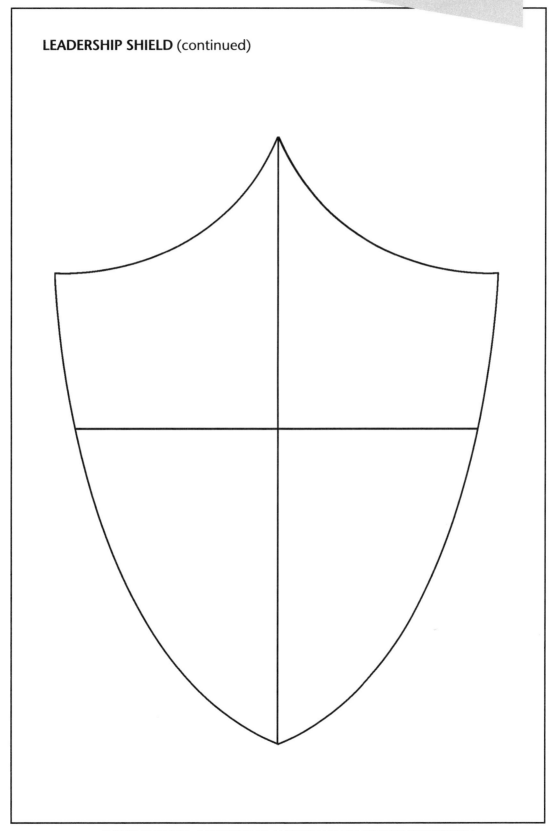

4

MAKE IT RHYME WITH "LEADER"

Overview of Activity

By writing a poem as a way to stretch one's creativity, leadership concepts are explored and encouraged.

Objectives

→ To focus participants on the topic of leadership.

→ To give participants an opportunity to become acquainted and begin working together.

→ To stimulate creative thinking.

Setting Up the Activity

GROUP SIZE
Up to 20 participants

ESTIMATED TIME
30 minutes

TRAINING METHODS
Creative writing

MATERIALS
None

EQUIPMENT AND SUPPLIES
Paper
Pens or pencils
100 index cards for each group
Flipchart

ROOM SET-UP
Tables and chairs for small groups of 3 to 5 people

Comments

Some participants will not be confident that they can accomplish this task. Use it to show them how to tap into their creative side and stretch themselves. This activity can be done in small groups or on an individual basis. If the latter, then each person would require a full deck of cards.

Trainer's Notes for Activity 4

STEP-BY-STEP PROCEDURE

Step 1: Divide participants into small groups of 3 to 5 people each. Hand each group a pack of index cards and one sheet of paper.

Step 2: Say, "Thinking about leadership in various ways can be instructive. If we stretch our imaginations, which often takes a linear form, we can discover fresh, new perspectives about our leadership strengths and challenges that will astonish us."'

Step 3: Give the following directions:

"Your group will be creating a personal leadership "deck" of words or terms that fit the categories listed on the flipchart.You can work from the sheet of paper and then transfer one word to each card, or you can write directly on the cards. Decide this before beginning."

Step 4: Your flipchart should show the following three categories:

➔ The Five Senses (sight, touch, taste, sound, smell)
(16 words for each of the five senses = 80)

➔ Motion (10 words)

➔ Abstractions (10 "abstractions," such as leadership, love, freedom, meaning of life)

Step 5: Then explain the rules. All words or terms on the list must be:

    ➔ Meaningful to you
    ➔ Specific (not "tree," but "aspen tree"; not "bird," but "robin")
    ➔ Pleasing to the ear

Use no adverbs and no plurals.

Step 6: Begin the poetry part of the activity with this explanation:

"When you have 100 words or terms written on the cards, spread them out. Choose cards that you can use to create a poem about leadership. Take 15 to 20 minutes to write a poem that supports the theme of leadership. Add more words as needed to flesh out the poem."

Offer the participants the following as an example of a poem:

Why does leadership make me think of bright, white light?
Is it the leader's clarity I feel as comfort?
The leader is a beacon through the night.
Is it the leader's gentle pressure I feel as comfort?

When I think of Leadership, it is a fresh, fragrant flag.
Is it the leader's support that gives me comfort?
The leader beckons and make me glad.
Is it their insistent, but gentle, speech that gives me comfort?

Comfort to follow; comfort to grow.
I am glad my Leader is in the know.

Step 7: When the groups have finished, have one member of each group read their poem to the total group. Encourage applause.

Step 8: Post the poems (or collect them and make copies for everyone) and bring the session to a close. The trainer concludes the activity by congratulating all the burgeoning poets and suggesting that they think about leadership as involving every sense and feeling identified in their poems.

POST-ACTIVITY REVIEW

Take time shortly after conducting this activity to reflect on how it went, how engaged the participants were, and what questions they raised. Then, make notes that include how much time you actually spent on the activity.

5

MEET MY LEADER

An Orange?

Overview of Activity

This activity helps the leader practice using analogies to describe various components of leadership.

Objectives

→ To use analogy to describe leaders.
→ To encourage participants to use all the human senses.

Setting Up the Activity

GROUP SIZE
Up to 20 participants

ESTIMATED TIME
30 minutes

TRAINING METHODS
→ Analogy
→ Discussion
→ Hands-on activity

MATERIALS
None

EQUIPMENT AND SUPPLIES
One interesting object per group, such as an orange or other fruit, an unusual box, a feather, an intriguing hat.

ROOM SET-UP
Chairs arranged in a circle

Comments

The concept of leadership is a complex one. This activity helps participants explore various facets of leadership. The use of objects to develop an analogy just creates more fun.

Trainer's Notes for Activity 5

STEP-BY-STEP PROCEDURE

Step 1: Select objects as noted. Have enough objects available so each group can have one object.

Step 2: Divide participants into groups of five (if you formed IDEA teams, they would do this together). Set up individual groups in circles.

Step 3: Explain that it is sometimes easier to describe leaders by using an analogy. Give the first object to each group. Ask participants to handle the object and to answer these questions within their group:

a. How does the object "feel" like a leader?
b. How does the object "see" like a leader?
c. How does the object "smell" like a leader?
d. How does the object "hear" like a leader?

For example, if they object was a feather, the responses to the above questions might be:

a. The leader uses his or her soft side when empathy and understanding is needed.

b. The leader can see the big picture by looking through and between the individual feathers.

c. The leader has none!

d. The leader listens to whose who are quiet as the winds of change blow the feather.

Step 4: Trade objects among the groups and repeat Step 3.

Step 5: Reassemble into one large group, and pose the following questions for discussion and debriefing:

a. What were the distinguishing features of your objects?

b. Which object best applies to your own leader or manager?

c. Because we cannot go around "touching" other people to become acquainted, how can we learn about others' uniqueness? Use the analogy in this activity to facilitate the identification of many qualities you find in yourself and your managers.

VARIATION

Pass around another object and ask participants to use it to describe themselves.

POST-ACTIVITY REVIEW

Take time shortly after conducting this activity to reflect on how it went, how engaged the participants were, and what questions they raised. Then, make notes that include how much time you actually spent on the activity.

6

TELL A STORY AND MAKE YOUR POINT!

Overview of Activity

Storytelling is a useful leadership competency; this activity provides practice for the participants.

Objectives

→ To identify the importance of storytelling as a leadership competency.
→ To demonstrate how to tell a story.
→ To practice telling a story.

Setting Up the Activity

GROUP SIZE
Up to 20 participants

ESTIMATED TIME
Set aside 15 minutes to demonstrate storytelling; 5 minutes for each person to tell a story; 10 minutes to debrief.

TRAINING METHODS
→ Presentation
→ Discussion
→ Storytelling

MATERIALS
Handout 6.1: *Storytelling Checklist*

EQUIPMENT AND SUPPLIES
Flipcharts and markers

ROOM SET-UP
Have participants sit in a circle in front of a fireplace, if possible. Otherwise, place chairs in a "U" shape.

Comments

This activity works well at the beginning of a leadership program. If you plan to have participants give presentations later on, this activity will help participants practice making impromptu presentations. Use it after your introduction and overview of the workshop agenda.

Resources

Read more about storytelling in *Encouraging the Heart,* written by Jim Kouzes and Barry Posner (see Chapter 8, pp. 99–106).

Trainer's Notes for Activity 6

STEP-BY-STEP PROCEDURE

Step 1: As the trainer, you need to model this skill of storytelling. Use Handout 6.1, *Storytelling Checklist,* as your guide to write a story. Practice your story out loud several times so you can tell it without notes. Before the class, tell your story that includes all the elements of a good story. You can choose either option below; note that the second option is appropriate because participants will be reviewing their skills and career goals throughout most of the leadership program.

Option 1: Tell the story about how the vision of the company or program became a reality.

Option 2: Tell a story about one of the trainers that highlights the struggle and lessons learned during his/her career.

Step 2: Present the elements of a good story.

Distribute Handout 6.1: *Storytelling Checklist,* and discuss the point.

Use the story you shared in Step 1 to review the elements of a good story.

Step 3: Have participants tell their own stories.

The task for each person is to tell a story. Select from topics such as these:

→ Tell a story about a time when you led at your best. (Note: Use this topic if you plan to use the Kouzes and Posner leadership model, because this was the basis of their research.)

→ Tell a story about the time in your life when you realized you were competent.

→ Tell a story about a time when you realized you could achieve a milestone in your career.

→ Tell a story about a time when you solved an important business problem.

Allow participants time to select a personal story and organize the points.

Step 4: Have participants decide the order in which they will tell their stories and then begin the storytelling session. Keep each story to approximately five minutes.

Step 5: Discuss the importance of storytelling as a leadership skill. Try to get each person to share what they think the value of storytelling is, using the following trigger questions:

→ How did family stories (or the lack of them) affect you as you were growing up?

→ What stories were told to you as a new employee in your company? Did these stories change your impression of the company? If so, how?

Summarize and discuss how storytelling can be used by aspiring leaders.

Ask participants to select a story frequently told in their organization, and retell it by following the outline covered in Step 2.

OR

Ask participants to write a story that recognizes someone else's accomplishments. Suggest that they submit it later to their company newsletter, tell it during a staff meeting, or broadcast it via e-mail.

Ask participants how they plan to use storytelling throughout their leadership program and work life.

POST-ACTIVITY REVIEW

Take time shortly after conducting this activity to reflect on how it went, how engaged the participants were, and what questions they raised. Then, make notes that include how much time you actually spent on the activity.

Storytelling Checklist

Telling a good story is easy: All you have to do is remember to include all these elements, in order. Use this handy checklist.

☐ Paint the scene. Tell where and when this story occurred.

☐ Identify the characters or people in your story. Give them names.

☐ State their predicament or problem.

☐ Clarify the characters' intentions. What went through their minds as they tried to handle the problem?

☐ Describe their actions. What did each person do? Be specific.

☐ Include "props" that help provide important details and help the listeners get into the story. A prop can be any item mentioned in your story. For example, if your story is about a time you helped your team through a crisis, you could hold up the frantic E-mails you received from them—and perhaps even read a short one.

☐ Include a surprise or element of amazement to make the story memorable. For example, using the story above, a prop could show a photo of the celebration you held for your team after the crisis was over.

☐ Tell how it ended.

7

TAKE TIME TO "JOURNAL"

Overview of Acvitity

This activity introduces the concept of journal writing and provides a reflection opportunity to that participants can acknowledge what they have learned and how they will continue to challenge themselves.

Objectives

→ To introduce the practice of writing down one's private thoughts and feelings

→ To encourage reflection on what was learned

→ To challenge oneself to learn in new ways

Setting Up the Activity

GROUP SIZE
Up to 20 participants

ESTIMATED TIME
30 minutes

TRAINING METHODS
→ Presentation
→ Reflection
→ Journal writing

MATERIALS
Enough bound paper for each person to create a journal, or individual spiral notebook.

EQUIPMENT AND SUPPLIES
None

ROOM SET-UP
Tables and chairs in any arrangement

Comments

Use the information below as the basis for any opening remarks you make as facilitator of the workshop. Be sure to explain that journaling is a great opportunity to assess our own performance, gauge learning, and integrate that learning into our activities.

Journal writing and storytelling are excellent ways to capture ideas for later use. Sometimes journal notations provide the basis for a story. Other times, hearing a story reminds the leader to record in his or her journal any reactions or responses that should be given additional thought.

The challenge in this activity is to teach the essentials of a very useful but private reflective practice within an open, shared session, as well as to generate enthusiasm for doing it after the session is over.

Trainer's Notes for Activity 7

STEP-BY-STEP PROCEDURE

Step 1: Introduce the subject of journaling and provide an overview of the activity.

For a long time, professionals in some disciplines have used journaling as an active recall process. Actors and directors are especially devoted to this technique. New actors are encouraged to write their ideas and feelings (free-flow) for at least 20 minutes a day. In this way, they develop a personal journal that captures an array of moods and emotions that can later be drawn on as they prepare for different character roles "for a long time."

As a leader, you are not really playing a character, but you are, in a real sense, orchestrating the team to work together to solve a business need or problem. A journal provides a personal and private way to track your great moments. If you use it regularly, you will capture your greatest successes, but—most importantly—you will also be recording those times when your choices weren't the best. New strategies and tactics can later be deduced from these writings.

Journaling is an important part of reflection, especially in adult learning. Adults learn best and have better retention when they consciously take time to reflect on their learning. A journal can help to trace changes in one's thinking over time. Journaling can also be guided, with questions provided from an outside source.

Step 2: Have participants practice journaling by explaining the basics.

→ Distribute the paper or individual spiral notebooks that will serve as their leadership journals.

→ Give participants 10 minutes to identify three things they learned about leadership that day and to how these will help them change a current practice. These thoughts should be recorded in their journal immediately.

→ Ask the group to think of "prompts" that can get the members started writing in their journals—things that will make the process comfortable and meaningful. For example, *How are you doing emotionally?* or *What aha! moment did I have during this session?* are good prompts that can be written in the front of their journals.

Step 3: Review the following journaling basics:

→ It is best to write the journal entry immediately, without worrying about every detail.

→ Set up a regular time to write in your journal.

→ Your experiences and your thoughts will help you understand your own behavior.

If you get "stuck" during your regular journal time, just write whatever comes to mind. Then, later on, re-read what you wrote and reflect on why you are stuck at this particular time.

Step 4: There will be points during this leadership program when we will ask you to add thoughts to this journal, so be sure to bring it to every session. Also, use the journal at work to jot down more observations about leadership—yours and others.

POST-ACTIVITY REVIEW

Take time shortly after conducting this activity to reflect on how it went, how engaged the participants were, and what questions they raised. Then, make notes that include how much time you actually spent on the activity.

8

THE LEADERSHIP PUZZLE

Overview of Activity

This activity incorporates visual imagery and encourages the leadership participants to use a symbol to represent their leadership program.

Objectives

→ To create a symbol for everything participants learn and to understand how it all fits together.

→ To show how ritual and memory joggers can be used to reinforce what has been learned and help make learning an ongoing process.

→ To apply what has been learned in the workshop.

Setting Up the Activity

GROUP SIZE
Up to 20 participants

ESTIMATED TIME
20 minutes

TRAINING METHODS
→ Visual imagery
→ Use of rituals

MATERIALS

Select one visual image that represents the leadership program, the organization, or an industry. Suggestions include:

→ A visual representation of the company's logo or headquarters in the background, and the words representing the modules in your program in the foreground.

→ An illustration or photograph of leaders (women and men), across which are printed the titles of the program modules.

The chosen visual image should be enlarged to approximately the size of a placemat. Then, mount it on cardboard and cut it into fairly large "puzzle" pieces.

EQUIPMENT AND SUPPLIES

None

ROOM SET-UP

Flexible, as long as the puzzle frame can remain in a fixed place throughout the workshop.

Comments

This idea works well if your leadership program is organized into several modules or will extend over a period of days. Each piece of the puzzle can represent one module or one day.

Trainer's Notes for Activity 8

STEP-BY-STEP PROCEDURE

Step 1: Introduce the puzzle to participants at the beginning of the leadership program. Show it first as an assembled whole, and then place the pieces in a bag. Keep the puzzle frame on display in the room throughout the workshop or program, so each added piece is visible to all.

Step 2: At the end of each module or training day, one piece will be added to the puzzle. Select one of these two ways to do this.

→ Ask for a volunteer to select the piece that will be added and to explain why she/he selected that one.

→ As facilitator, select the piece that represents the module just completed, and add it to the puzzle.

Step 3: At the end of your leadership program, give each participant a smaller version of the puzzle (or a plaque with the picture of the puzzle on it) as a way of reminding them of what they learned about leadership.

POST-ACTIVITY REVIEW

Take time shortly after conducting this activity to reflect on how it went, how engaged the participants were, and what questions they raised. Then, make notes that include how much time you actually spent on the activity.

9

THE EXHIBIT HALL

Overview of Activity

This opportunity provides an opportunity for each participant to highlight a strength or competency that would be useful to others. Each person prepares an exhibit banner that identifies the thrust of his or her idea. All are encouraged to walk from display to display and identify those people with whom they might interact at a later time.

Objectives

→ To provide an ice-breaking opportunity to get acquainted and share resources.

→ To demonstrate that each individual is an expert at something.

Setting Up the Activity

GROUP SIZE
Minimum of 20 participants

ESTIMATED TIME
30 minutes to 1 hour

TRAINING METHODS
→ Demonstration
→ Presentation

MATERIALS
None, except what participants bring to display

EQUIPMENT AND SUPPLIES
→ Tables and tablecloths
→ Poster board and markers (for signs)
→ Name tags with "Exhibitor" ribbons attached

ROOM SET-UP
→ Ample wall space
→ Tables and chairs arranged for easy movement of people (to view exhibits)

Comments

Use this activity to emphasize that each participant comes to the program with ideas and experiences regarding leadership. The Exhibit Hall will give them the opportunity to share this expertise. Use this activity when you have sufficient space to display exhibits.

Trainer's Notes for Activity 9

STEP-BY-STEP PROCEDURE

Step 1: When participants preregister for the session or multiday workshop, instruct them to bring in items at a designated time for an exhibit based on participant experiences and skills in leadership. Give them a written sheet with examples of what you mean, such as:

– A collection of articles or books on the subject that they found useful.

– Several performance-evaluation forms they have used or find interesting.

– A step-by-step approach to writing reports.

– Their best idea for. . . . (with a written description).

– A how-to demonstration of a skill.

– A PowerPoint presentation on a leadership topic.

- A video they use to teach employees a skill, along with points for discussion.

- Posters showing a team celebrating an achievement.

Explain at preregistration that participants will be setting up an exhibit. Each person should prepare a banner or poster and bring all the equipment and supplies they need to make their part of the exhibit attractive and inviting.

Step 2: As each person arrives for the exhibit session, give them a name tag with an "Exhibitor" ribbon attached. Assign each individual a specific table or wall space for his or her items. Provide the group with materials for exhibit signs that show each person's name and organizational affiliation.

Step 3: When all of the exhibits are set up, invite people to mingle and network in the Exhibit Hall (refreshments optional). Suggest that participants note the names of anyone with whom they are interested in having an extended conversation.

Step 4: Ask the following questions:

1. What was the most useful exhibit—one that gave you ideas you can use?

2. Whom did you meet that you would want to meet again?

3. What suggestions do you have for "saving" these exhibits, so we can return to them later on?

POST-ACTIVITY REVIEW

Take time shortly after conducting this activity to reflect on how it went, how engaged the participants were, and what questions they raised. Then, make notes that include how much time you actually spent on the activity.

10

WALK AND TALK

Overview of Activity

This exercise is useful after lunch, as it provides an appropriate physical activity during which one reivews what has been learned and explores what other leadership competencies will be presented.

Objectives

→ To review what individuals have learned so far in the workshop.
→ To identify what else needs to be accomplished,
→ To provide physical exercise and an opportunity to reenergize.

Setting Up the Activity

GROUP SIZE
Any number of participants, divided into pairs

ESTIMATED TIME
20 minutes

TRAINING METHODS
→ Movement
→ Discussion

MATERIALS
None

EQUIPMENT AND SUPPLIES
Flipchart and markers

ROOM SET-UP
Chairs arranged in a circle or facing the front (for discussion)

Comments

This activity is especially useful after a meal, because it requires a short walk. Participants have an opportunity to review what they have learned and to share with the trainer what they still hope to learn from the workshop before it ends.

Trainer's Notes for Activity 10

STEP-BY-STEP PROCEDURE

Step 1: Divide participants into pairs of individuals who are not well acquainted.

Step 2: Write these three questions on the flipchart:

➔ What is the most significant thing you have learned so far in this workshop?

➔ What analogy can you make between what you see as you walk around and the goals of this workshop?

➔ What else do you still want to learn in this workshop?

Step 3: Instruct participants to take a 15-minute walk in their designated pairs, during which they discuss these three questions. Tell them to be sure that each person in the pair takes a total of seven minutes to answer the questions. In other words, see that the "talk" time is equal.

Step 4: When they return, ask each participant to share something he or she has learned from their walking partners.

Step 5: Ask volunteers to express what they or their partners want from the rest of the workshop.

Step 6: During this leadership program, we will use your ideas and suggestions.

POST-ACTIVITY REVIEW

Take time shortly after conducting this activity to reflect on how it went, how engaged the participants were, and what questions they raised. Then, make notes that include how much time you actually spent on the activity.

11

THE KOOSH BALL REVIEW GAME

Overview of Activity

In this energizing activity, partipants throw and catch a large koosh ball as they ask or answer questions relating to leadership.

Objectives

➔ To review key concepts or information.
➔ To have fun.

Setting Up the Activity

WHEN TO USE

Use this game at each major junction in your workshop, or when you want to review what participants have learned. You can play the game at the end of one segment or use it as a warm-up at the beginning of the next session.

GROUP SIZE

Up to 20 participants

ESTIMATED TIME

10 minutes

TRAINING METHODS
→ Application
→ Game
→ Hands-on activity

MATERIALS
Buy a Koosh ball—the rubber ball that looks like porcupine needles—or a soft rubber ball approximately the size of a baseball.

EQUIPMENT AND SUPPLIES
Koosh ball (larger ones work best)

ROOM SET-UP
Enough open space for participants to stand in a circle

Comments

This activity adds the element of competition to the leadership program and will help the facilitator determine if participants have learned what has been presented so far.

Trainer's Notes for Activity 11

STEP-BY-STEP PROCEDURE

Step 1: Form a circle with participants, leaving enough room to throw a ball back and forth. Participants should stand with their hands to their sides.

Step 2: Throw the Koosh ball to a participant and ask a quiz question. (If the ball falls to the floor, give it to the person at whom it was aimed.) If the answer is incorrect, retrieve the ball and throw it to someone else so they can answer the question. If the answer is correct, the participant can throw the ball to someone who hasn't answered a question.

Step 3: Keep throwing the ball with every new question until each participant has answered at least one question correctly.

Step 4: Remind the participants that a review is valuable because it means they are more likely to retain and apply what they've learned. This could be a good time to remind them to write some reflections in their journals.

VARIATION

Have each participant write down two or three questions for the facilitator to ask.

SAMPLE QUESTIONS

Create a list of questions based on what you covered in the last segment of your workshop. Here are some examples:

→ Who traveled the farthest to get to this workshop?

→ Why is it important to identify the expertise and resources within your team or staff?

→ Explain one difference between a group and a team.

→ Why are the best leaders flexible?

→ Explain one distinction between a leader and a manager.

→ Name two qualities that a leader should develop.

→ When should a leader empower others?

POST-ACTIVITY REVIEW

Take time shortly after conducting this activity to reflect on how it went, how engaged the participants were, and what questions they raised. Then, make notes that include how much time you actually spent on the activity.

12

I LEARNED A LOT!

Overview of Activity

The participants summarize their leadership learnings through round-robin discussion and responses to questions asked by the facilitator.

Objectives

→ To clarify what participants have personally learned and are willing to share with the group.

→ To provide an opportunity to review the day's topics.

→ To summarize thoughts and feelings.

→ To articulate ideas with clarity.

Setting-Up the Activity

GROUP SIZE
Up to 20 participants

ESTIMATED TIME
This will vary, depending on the size of your group. Two minutes per participant is a good average.

TRAINING METHODS
→ Round-robin discussion
→ Reflection

MATERIALS
One 4" × 6" index card for each person, preprinted with the text shown below. Use colored cards (especially the vivid ones) to add a sense of festivity.

I learned that _____.

I re-learned that _____.

I discovered that _____.

I noticed that _____.

I was surprised that _____.

I am disappointed that _____.

I plan to _____.

EQUIPMENT AND SUPPLIES
None

ROOM SET-UP
Chairs arranged in a circle

Comment

This activity serves a similar purpose to that of the Koosh Ball Game—to help participants re-focus on what was covered in a particular activity or perhaps a segment of the overall leadership program. A review of lessons helps reinforce learning—and thus enhances retention.

Resource

This exercise was adapted from an activity used in Lois Hart's book *Connections.* The exercise is an excellent way to involve all participants and bring a workshop in which you must cover many topics to a satisfying close.

Trainer's Notes for Activity 12

STEP-BY-STEP PROCEDURE

Step 1: Introduce the activity by saying, "We've all had an intense day. As one way of personally evaluating our time together, let's share with one another some of what we have learned. We will do this by focusing on answers to "sentence stems."

Step 2: Pass out one preprinted index card to each person and explain the procedure. Say,

"We'll go around the circle and hear answers to each stem, one at a time. Each person should respond.

Of course, if a stem does not resonate with you, then feel free to pass or provide a stem that more clearly expresses what you wish to share.

Focus on what you have learned about leadership *today.*"

Participants must not comment on what others say. As facilitator, your role should be to thank each person for each contribution. Don't elaborate on what they say.

Step 3: Thank you for your contributions. I suggest you record your leaning in your journal. As we adjourn (for a break, lunch, or the session), you might want to talk further with anyone whose "I learned. . . ." resonated with you.

POST-ACTIVITY REVIEW

Take time shortly after conducting this activity to reflect on how it went, how engaged the participants were, and what questions they raised. Then, make notes that include how much time you actually spent on the activity.

13

WORD SCRAMBLE CLOSURE GAME

Overview of Activity

As a closing activity, this game reviews concepts that realte to the skills demonstrated in the leadership workshop. Working in teams—and against a clock—the features of the skill are "unscrambled" from pre-made cards.

Objectives

→ To review key concepts learned in the leadership workshop.
→ To have fun while closing a workshop or program.

Setting Up the Activity

GROUP SIZE
Any number of teams of six (one person per team acts as Game Monitor)

ESTIMATED TIME
20 minutes

TRAINING METHODS
→ Application
→ Game

MATERIALS
Ten index cards per group, each card bearing a different leadership concept or skill (word or short phrase—the letters must be scrambled).

EQUIPMENT AND SUPPLIES
None

ROOM SET-UP
Tables and chairs

Comments

This activity adds the element of competition, so give a prize to the team that successfully unscrambles all of its words first. It is also a way to be sure that participants have learned what is being presented in the leadership workshop.

ADVANCE PREPARATION
Select up to ten words that represent key ideas or skills presented during your leadership workshop. For each word, write the letters on a card, but scramble them up. Clip each set of scrambled-word cards togetherand make sure you have a set of ten for each table group. Here are some suggested words to use:

Leadership	Ethics
Manager	Balance
Flexibility	Conflict
Style	Negotiate
Trust	Coach
Power	Celebrate

Trainer's Notes for Activity 13

STEP-BY-STEP PROCEDURE

Step 1: Divide participants into teams of six (use the same work groups you have used for other workshop activities, if you wish). Assign the role of Game Monitor to one member of each team. This person stands at the end of the table.

Step 2: Explain how the game is played, using the following guidelines:

One set of scrambled-word cards is placed in the middle of each group's table. When the game starts, the first person to the right of the Game Monitor selects one card from the pile and tries to identify the correct word, using all the scrambled letters on the card.

Set a time limit of two minutes to unscramble each word. If the individual can't identify the correct word, the other group members can help.

When someone has identified the word correctly, the Game Monitor signals the facilitator and asks the participant to explain how the word relates to an important leadership skill.

Repeat this process until each person in each group unscrambles a word and defines it correctly.

Step 3: Award a prize to the team that is first to unscramble all ten words. The prize might be that they are first in line for lunch or it might be a bowl of a special snack or a small gift for each person. Thank everyone for their efforts to unscramble the leadership words.

POST-ACTIVITY REVIEW

Take time shortly after conducting this activity to reflect on how it went, how engaged the participants were, and what questions they raised. Then, make notes that include how much time you actually spent on the activity.

14

DEAR DIARY . . .

Overview of Activity

This engaging activity helps participants see that leadership growth is like taking a journey. The participants move from place to place within the room and describe through oral, written, or hands-on activities, how their own leadership journey is developing.

Objectives

➔ To review what participants have learned in the workshop.

➔ To provide time to reflect on what has been learned and record important learnings or observations.

Setting Up the Activity

GROUP SIZE
Up to 20 participants

ESTIMATED TIME
Allow 5 minutes to introduce the activity; 6 minutes to get through each station; and 2 to 3 minutes for each person to share their entries at the end.

TRAINING METHODS
→ Application
→ Reflection
→ Journal writing
→ Use of Metaphors
→ Round-robin discussion

MATERIALS
→ Handout 14.1: *Travel Diary Station Descriptions* for each station
→ Table tents for names of each station
→ A diary or journal for each participant

EQUIPMENT AND SUPPLIES
Each station, as identified below, should be equipped with the following props:

Station 1, Starting Point of Journey: binoculars, itinerary or workshop agenda, airline ticket, maps

Station 2, Traveling Companions: photo of class participants

Station 3, Corporate Jungle: box with large key, toy monkey, fake palm tree, toy snake or tiger

Station 4, Sea of Change: small model or toy boat

Station 5, River of Risk: simulate a river with blue tape, bowl of water with small boat, picture of dangerous river

Station 6, Coach Ville: photo of workshop facilitator

Station 7, City of Politics: newspaper photo of known politicians or picture of members of Congress

Station 8, Village of Networking: collage of people's faces or several small dolls to represent people in their network

Station 9, Pinnacle Peak: Small flag labeled "Success" or date of workshop completion

For the whole room: Tape Recorder or CD player, and soft music.

ROOM SET-UP
Nine small tables with two chairs per table. Spread out the tables within the room. For the summary phase, have enough space for a circle of chairs. (Note: Place additional chairs at the stations if the group is larger than nine.)

Comments

We use metaphors throughout our leadership programs as a way to teach a concept or reinforce learning more effectively. Metaphors also provide visual representations or props that offer a tangible connection with what we are presenting. This closure activity capitalizes on those metaphors.

We think that it is imperative to set aside a significant block of time to bring closure to the participants' learning experience.

Our examples outlined in this activity fit what we teach in our leadership program. Please adapt our examples to fit the content you cover in your own leadership training.

Set up stations when participants are not present. It will take about 10 to 15 minutes, so send them on a break if you need to.

We have included sample instructions for nine workstations. At each station, there should be a sign labeling the station, props for the metaphor, and a handout for that station.

Trainer's Notes for Activity 14

VARIATION

Consider adding stations that require participants to do more than simply talk and write, such as a station where they can work on an art project or choose music to match an achievement or a goal.

STEP-BY-STEP PROCEDURE

Step 1: Introduce the topic by saying, "This activity acts as a reminder of where you have been and where you want to go. It uses active journal writing. This has been a heady journey; we have navigated a sea of change, and many surprises are ahead."

Explain the directions, by saying, "You will move through nine stations, staying at each one for approximately 6 minutes. The task for each station is written on a handout at the station."

When you complete the task, wait for the signal to move. Be sure to take your notes with you when you move on. Examples of completed tasks are:

1. The first day of my leadership journey began at the moment I decided to attend this program. There I learned that I definitely wanted to learn the difference between my management skills and my leadership skills, so I could focus on the latter.

2. My traveling companions taught me that *they often experience the same challenges as I do as a leader.*

3. I demonstrated my authentic leadership self in the Corporate Jungle by *gaining the confidence to appropriately challenge issues based on my values.*

4. I navigated the Sea of Change successfully by *remembering that I can impact the change process so our team will successfully and positively complete the transition.*

5. When crossing the River of Risk, I *now evaluate the level of the risk and plan accordingly, so I will succeed.*

6. At Coach Ville, I met my coach. What I took away was *the value of someone who objectively helps me evaluate my problems and encourages me when I lack confidence.*

7. During my stay in the City of Politics, I experienced *a definite Aha that I do use several types of power and that flexibility serves my interests.*

8. I greeted many other leaders at the Village of Networking. We shared *career tips, sources for information, even a dog sitter for when I'm traveling on business.*

9. At Pinnacle Peak, I knew I just had to pass the following leadership dimensions on to others: *they include clarification of values and vision, the benefits of regularly recognizing others and celebrating more often, handling conflicts, and strategic planning.*

Step 2: Show participants how they will rotate to all stations.

Hand out one slip of paper to each person that identifies the station he or she should visit first. Each person should begin with a different number.

Play soft music in the background.

Every six minutes, call "time." Ask everyone to move to the next numbered station with their journal.

Step 3: When everyone has completed all nine stations, place chairs in a circle and facilitate a round-robin discussion. Each person should share highlights and important ideas gleaned from the experience.

Step 4: You have completed this particular journey to learn more about leadership. Your travel to each of these nine stations has helped you complete a review of what you have learned and to establish some goals for the future. Remember that success is not measured by a specific destination but by the distance you have traveled. Bon Voyage!

POST-ACTIVITY REVIEW

Take time shortly after conducting this activity to reflect on how it went, how engaged the participants were, and what questions they raised. Then, make notes that include how much time you actually spent on the activity.

Travel Diary
Station Descriptions

Dear Travel Diary:
The first day of my leadership journey began at the _____ .
There I learned. . . .

Dear Travel Diary:
My traveling companions taught me that. . . .

Dear Travel Diary:
I demonstrated my authentic leadership self in the Corporate
Jungle by. . . .

Dear Travel Diary:
I navigated the Sea of Change successfully by. . . .

Dear Travel Diary:
When crossing the River of Risk, I. . . .

Dear Travel Diary:
At Coach Ville, I met my coach. What I took away was. . . .

Dear Travel Diary:
During my stay in the City of Politics, I experienced. . . .

Dear Travel Diary:
I greeted many other leaders at the Village of Networking. We shared. . . .

Dear Travel Diary:
At Pinnacle Peak, I knew I just had to pass the following leadership
dimensions on to others:

15

LET'S MEET SOON!
Forming Professional Resource Groups

Overview of Activity

This plan can be followed if participants want to meet and continue exploring learning opportunities after the formal classes have ended.

Objectives

→ To review the advantages of forming a professional group of peers.
→ To identify the steps and guidelines used by such groups.
→ To facilitate the creation of a resource group.

Setting Up the Activity

GROUP SIZE
Up to 20 participants

ESTIMATED TIME
1 to 2 hours

TRAINING METHODS
→ Presentation
→ Discussion

MATERIALS
Handout 15.1: *Guidelines and Tips for Success* (add to it as appropriate).

EQUIPMENT AND SUPPLIES
None

ROOM SET-UP
Chairs arranged in a circle

Comments

Learning does not end when the workshop is over, but leaders do forget some of what they learned as they return to their busy work lives. A professional resource group made up of peers provides a regular forum in which to extend learning, share successes, and solve professional problems.

This activity provides your participants with an opportunity to create such a group with people they already know. Participants have shared similar learning experiences through your workshop module or series. This is a great foundation for creating a successful resource group.

Trainer's Notes for Activity 15

STEP-BY-STEP PROCEDURE

Step 1: Provide an overview of the concept by suggesting that participants face a dilemma: Once the workshop is over, they will return to their everyday responsibilities and are likely to neglect some or all of their good intentions to apply what they have learned. Ask volunteers to share how this can happen.

Introduce this scenario: At work, they run across a problem that appears unsolvable. They find themselves wishing that someone else—perhaps from the workshop—was around to help them think through the problem. Ask participants to talk about how often they think this might happen.

Step 2: Introduce the idea of forming a professional resource group—a group of peers who meet regularly to discuss common issues, help one another solve work problems, celebrate successes, and extend learning.

Ask if any participants have been members of such a group. Discuss their experiences as you go over the steps involved in forming a professional group.

Step 3: Forming a Professional Group

1. Gather 4 to 6 individuals who are committed to making this idea a reality. Try to have some diversity of background, skills, and attitudes.

2. Agree on a time and place for the first meeting. Allow approximately two hours for that session.

3. At the first meeting, each person shares what she or he wants from participation in the group. Keep notes for future reference.

4. Members discuss and reach consensus on the purpose of the group, perhaps even creating a mission statement.

5. Members agree on a name for the group. (Have fun doing this!)

6. Distribute Handout 15.1 Together, discuss guidelines for your group. Examples include:

   – We will openly contribute what we know and think.

   – We will attend all of the meetings.

   – We will take time to prepare for our meetings.

   – We will freely share ideas, resources, and materials with one another.

   – We will help each other solve problems.

7. Select someone to host the next meeting, and send out reminders and directions.

   Select another member of the group to be the facilitator. (Consider rotating this role.)

8. Review the following suggestions for subsequent meetings of the group.

   Rotate the location of meetings. Some groups meet at each other's offices, while others meet at restaurants or in their homes. The host plans the food and sends out reminders.

   Rotate the facilitator at each meeting. This person sets the agenda, keeps the discussion on track, makes sure everyone has a chance to participate, and keeps track of the time.

Identify topics for discussion that members want to cover at upcoming meetings. Individuals volunteer to prepare a presentation or questions that will help group members delve deeper into the topic.

Set aside time at the beginning of each meeting to let people share successes and other good news.

Periodically conduct a team-building activity.

9. Share these additional tips for success:

Avoid allowing outsiders to attend, unless they are needed as presenters.

On a quarterly basis, evaluate how the group is functioning. Review what you have discussed and accomplished in the recent meetings. Review your purpose and guidelines and update as needed.

You will find that some individuals will want or need to drop out because of other commitments or a shift in their professional goals. It is important that others in the group understand and not resent this change. Be sure to recognize this person's contributions at their final meeting.

Consider naming a replacement. This is difficult on the remaining group members as well as someone new because the group now has a shared history. It is possible to make this transition, however. Review the criteria for membership, and brainstorm to come up with a list of individuals who meet the criteria. Assign someone to give the new person some background on group members, review the guidelines, and explain anything else that will help him or her integrate.

Step 4: Begin establishing the group. Explain that there are several ways to form the group. For example, if you used "work teams" in the workshop for portions of your modules, ask those people if they'd like to continue as a group.

Another way is to ask participants to state the kind of group they would like to be in, such as, "Others in my telecommunications industry," "Others who work in my part of the city," or "A group of only women." Some people might wish to form a group around a specific topic or issue. Once individuals explain what they are proposing, consider having the rest of the participants get together with the person making the proposal closest to their needs.

Once the groups are formed, provide time for each group to either go through the steps outlined in Step 2, or at least to set the time and place for their first meeting.

Step 5: This activity was inspired by a real-life experience in which the co-author of this book, Lois Hart, was involved. A group of six women, who all worked in the same profession, decided to form a support group. At the first meeting, she facilitated the discussion to hear what each person hoped to get out of the group.Based on that information, the members created their purpose and mission.

With those key items as the foundation, it was easier to complete some important details. They were familiar with team guidelines, so reaching consensus on this group's goals went quickly. The fun part was creating a name. They chose "Arriba," which means "go fast" or "hurry up" in Spanish.

They met every 4 to 6 weeks, rotating locations and always sharing a meal. Eventually, they lost two members because of illness and job change, but they were replaced. Arriba was definitely a success, as the members are still meeting after 11 years.

Now, you know how to start and maintain a professional support group. Let's work out a system so we can follow your success. I'd be willing to receive your updates and forward them on to your other colleagues.

POST-ACTIVITY REVIEW

Take time shortly after conducting this activity to reflect on how it went, how engaged the participants were, and what questions they raised. Then, make notes that include how much time you actually spent on the activity.

Guidelines and Tips for Success

➔ We will openly contribute what we know and think.

➔ We will attend all of the meetings.

➔ We will take time to prepare for our meetings.

➔ We will freely share ideas, resources, and materials with one another.

➔ We will help each other solve problems.

➔ Avoid allowing outsiders to attend, unless they are needed as presenters.

➔ On a quarterly basis, evaluate how the group is functioning. Review what you have discussed and accomplished in the recent meetings. Review your purpose and guidelines, and update as needed.

➔ You will find that some individuals will want or need to drop out due to other commitments or a shift in their professional goals. It is important that others in the group understand and not resent this change. Be sure to recognize this person's contributions at their final meeting.

➔ Consider naming a replacement. This is difficult on the remaining group members as well as someone new because the group now has a shared history. It is possible to make this transition, however. Review the criteria for membership, and brainstorm to come up with a list of individuals who meet the criteria. Assign someone to give the new person some background on group members, review the guidelines, and explain anything else that will help him or her integrate.

16

SAYING GOODBYE

Overview of Activity

Appreciation is a leadership competency that is often underutilized. The structure of this activity encourages appropriate and positive comments.

Objective

To provide an opportunity for workshop participants to express appreciation for the contributions of the other participants and their facilitators.

Setting Up the Activity

GROUP SIZE
Up to 20 participants

ESTIMATED TIME
➔ 10 minutes to introduce the activity
➔ Break time to write and put up comment slips
➔ 5 minutes at the end of the program

TRAINING METHOD
Personal reflection

MATERIALS

→ Five to seven sentence "stems" on a page cut into separate slips of paper (use brightly colored paper to make it more fun). Feel free to make up your own comment sheets. See Job Aid 16.1: *Appreciation Sentences* for samples to get started.

→ An 8½″ × 11″ sheet of paper for each participant and facilitator, preprinted with his or her name on it and some visual image that is appropriate for each person. (These should be hung around the room before the activity is announced.)

EQUIPMENT AND SUPPLIES

Tape

ROOM SET-UP

Flexible

Comments

Too often we rush the end of a program, tacking on the evaluation and hurrying through the goodbyes. This activity focuses on what individuals have learned and gained from one another, participant-to-participant and facilitator-to-participant.

The slips of paper with sentence stems need to be distributed several hours before the close of the workshop, but after the participants and the facilitators have been together long enough to gather perceptions about one another.

As you plan the ending of your program, put the evaluations and other housekeeping tasks first, so that you can end on a high note. This activity will ensure that participants leave with positive feelings about their experience.

Trainer's Notes for Activity 16

STEP-BY-STEP PROCEDURE

Step 1: Introduce the topic by saying:

"We believe it is important to reflect on what you learned from one another during this leadership program. As we wind up this workshop, let's also celebrate the experience."

Step 2: Give instructions for the activity, saying:

"I have here slips of paper, each with a different sentence stem. Please try to fill out one slip of paper for each person who impressed you, touched you, or left you with a good memory.

Fill out these comment slips throughout the remaining hours we have together. On the wall is a comment sheet for each participant. Tape each comment slip, one for each of your fellow participants, to each person's sheet."

Throughout the day, remind participants of this task.

Step 3: Complete closing tasks, including evaluations. Then ask each person to go to their "place" at the wall. With quiet music in the background, ask them to silently read and absorb what others have said about them.

When everyone is done reading, gather people into a circle. Ask participants to silently look at each person's face and express thanks with their eyes.

End with a cheer, such as

"*Lead on!*" or

"We can do it! We *have* done it! We *will* do it!"

Appreciation Sentences

Sent to _____

 You really made a difference by. . . .

Sent to _____

 I'm impressed with. . . .

Sent to _____

 You got my attention with. . . .

Sent to _____

 One of the things I enjoy most about you is. . . .

Sent to _____

I just wanted to let you know. . . .

APPRECIATION SENTENCES (continued)

Sent to _____

We couldn't have done it without you!

Sent to _____

What an effective way to . . . .

Sent to _____

The gift you have given me is . . . .

PART TWO

To Thine Own Self Be True

Leaders come to their positions with a great many skills, attitudes, values, experiences, and educational backgrounds. Highly effective leaders have in common a set of specific leadership competencies, which we will explore in this next section. We chose the title *To Thine Own Self Be True* because the activities focus on the development of the individual as leader.

This section begins with three assessments. The first, *Organizational Leadership,* assesses a leader's skills in six dimensions relative to his or her level in the organizational hierarchy. The second, *The Leadership Challenge,* provides an overview of an outstanding model of leadership competencies developed by Barry Posner and Jim Kouzes. The third uses a card-sort activity so that participants can learn the difference between management skills and leadership skills.

The next set of activities in this section can help leaders recognize the importance of maintaining a sense of adventure in their work and building a trusting relationship with the individuals they guide. All leaders need to explore how they respond to change so they will be able to help their own followers handle change. Before you can do that, however, you need to clarify your own values because values are the basis of ethical decisions. The activity *A Metaphor for Change* will help you do that. The exercise that comes next will help you solve ethical dilemmas using a step-by-step process.

Three activities address the subject of power. In the first, leaders complete a handout that helps identify their personal style of power. This is followed by a fun activity using a courtroom scenario that puts this knowledge into practice. An affirmation activity completes this trilogy on power.

Leaders should not be content to simply "work," as so many busy professionals are prone to do. They must reaffirm their need to create and maintain balance. We often turn to symbolism and metaphors in our training to explain how to do this. There are two activities that draw on these techniques to help leaders remember what they've learned about balance and identify ways to think about integrating professional development with activities from everyday life, such as gardening.

Part Two concludes with an interesting activity about the key skills savvy leaders use to enhance their careers.

17

ORGANIZATIONAL LEADERSHIP ASSESSMENT

Overview of Activity

This activity helps the leader identify his or her goals and the strengths they will build from, as they plan their leadership growth.

Objectives

→ To introduce the concept of Organizational Leadership.

→ To identify six dimensions of leadership.

→ To demonstrate how the skills in each competency vary according to job role or level of leadership.

→ To assess one's strengths and needs for present or future leadership positions.

→ To develop an action plan for professional development.

Setting Up the Activity

GROUP SIZE
Maximum of 10 participants per facilitator

ESTIMATED TIME
1 to 1½ hours

MATERIALS

→ A copy of Handout 17.1: *Organizational Leadership Assessment,* for each participant.

→ Handout 17.2: *A Plan for Leadership Development*

EQUIPMENT AND SUPPLIES
Flipchart
Room Set-Up
Tables and chairs

Comments

See Step-by-Step Procedure for important notes.

VARIATIONS

→ Distribute the instrument to all participants before presenting this module, so they have the opportunity to carefully complete it before the workshop.

→ Provide enough time in the workshop to cover all six dimensions in one sitting.

Trainer's Notes for Activity 17

STEP-BY-STEP PROCEDURE

Step 1: Explain that the Organizational Leadership model used for this activity separates the management staff into three levels:

Supervisory
Middle Management
Top Management

It organizes leader responsibilities into six dimensions or competencies:

Communication
Performance Management
Coaching and Counseling
Human Relations
Decision-Making
Planning

Step 2: Explain that the emphasis within each competency shifts as an individual moves up the leadership ladder. For example, a top manager or executive devotes more time to long-term planning and forecasting than a middle manager, who needs to focus on developing programs to implement the plans. Lower level supervisors, on the other hand, are responsible for executing the plans. All these activities lie within the planning dimension, but the focus is tied to each person's job role.

As leaders change levels, they must also change behaviors. This requires giving up some activities (even if they were good at them) to devote enough time to new leadership responsibilities.

Step 3: Distribute a copy of Handout 17.1 to each participant. Ask them to focus on a single competency, such as Communication. Explain how to read the matrix. As an example, choose one level (i.e., middle management) and review the skills generally required of leaders at that particular level.

Step 4: Ask participants to focus on the leadership position they currently hold as they complete this assessment.

Step 5: Coding directions for the assessment are as follows: "Read each leadership behavior or competency in the selected column. If you already possess or have mastered a skill, decide how strong you are in that skill. The rating code is:

+3   Perfected this skill and use it easily
+2   High degree of proficiency
+1   Some proficiency

If the skill needs to be developed, use this rating code:

−1   Needs some perfecting
−2   A lot of work is needed
−3   A completely undeveloped skill

Place your rating number to the left of the box showing each skill. Do not forget the plus (+) or minus (−) sign. For example, "+1 in Writing Reports."

Step 6: Once all participants have rated each item in the selected column, ask them to review all areas with a minus sign.

Step 7: Next, distribute Handout 17.2, and ask people to list up to three skills in the numbered spaces to the right of the competency. Explain that the columns marked "Strategies" and "Resources" are where they record ideas for achieving their development goals. Have the participants select a second competency that most interests them and follow the steps just outlined.

Step 8: Form groups with a maximum of five participants or have them gather into their already formed IDEA groups. Take 10 to 15 minutes to discuss their responses to the following questions:

➜ How accurately did the model fit what you actually do in your leadership position or what you imagine a person at that level should do?

➜ What did you observe about yourself? What surprised you? Explain what you mean.

➜ Based on your observations and your own plan, what are the implications for your leadership development?

Step 9: Reassemble into one large group, and ask a representative from each small group to summarize responses to the questions in Step 8.

Step 10: Then, address the issue of "overlap" between levels. For example, many participants will say that they don't seem to fit neatly into only one column—they use some skills from the supervisory, middle, and top-management categories. You will need to point out that in small organizations, where fewer people do all the work, or in new ones that have not clarified and institutionalized job roles, there will be an overlap of responsibility and instances where individual employees must take on tasks that go far beyond their defined roles.

Step 11: Next, explain that no human behavior is so cut and dried he or she can be classified into only one dimension. The leadership behaviors described in this model are often interrelated: Conflict resolution appearing under "Human Relations" might also be a component of "Counseling" or "Communication."

Step 12: Reinforce that leadership is complicated; it is made up of many skills and behaviors. The instrument is designed to make participants aware of these leadership skills. Reassure them that the purpose of the assessment is not to make them think they must possess all these skills, but rather to focus on the skills they will need to be an effective leader in the position they now hold.

Step 13: Remind participants that becoming a good leader takes time. As individuals, we change as we learn and grow. Because leadership opportunities and positions change, it is important to review one's leadership strengths and challenges on a regular basis. Complete a new self-assessment quarterly, bi-annually, or annually within a position, but also when you are considering a new leadership position.

Step 14: Summarize the original objectives for this activity and how you will use what participants learned about their own leadership skills in the remaining modules of your leadership program.

POST-ACTIVITY REVIEW

Take time shortly after conducting this activity to reflect on how it went, how engaged the participants were, and what questions they raised. Then, make notes that include how much time you actually spent on the activity.

Organizational Leadership Assessment

Skill Strength: +3 Perfected
+2 High but not perfected
+1 Some Proficiency

Development Needs: −1 Needs some work
−2 Needs much work
−3 Completely undeveloped

	Supervisor	Middle Manager	Top-Level Manager	Executive
Communication (Interpersonal)	— Listens empathetically in order to seek understanding.	— Listens to people in order to identify patterns of problems that impact organizational programs.	— Listens to people to identify patterns of problems that impact organizational policies.	— Listens to comprehend patterns of problems that impact organizational policies.
	— Uses persuasion.	— Uses influencing skills.	— Gives many reports and presentations.	— Gives many presentations.
	— Gives Feedback on employee performance.	— Sets up training on how to communicate feedback to employees.	— Allocates funds for training.	
	— Writes regular production or service reports to manager.	— Writes integrative reports for top management.	— Prepares reports to Board of Directors and government agencies.	— Signs reports to Board of Directors and government agencies.
		— Sets up training on how to write reports		

Communication (Intra-organizational)	— Manages e-mail. — Reads technical information. — Disseminates information sent to this level.	— Manages e-mail. — Reads reports and pertinent professional literature. — Develops systems or programs to enhance intra-organizational communication. — Collects and forwards information in both directions.	— Sets policy about e-mail. — Reads reports and pertinent professional literature. — Recommends systems or programs to enhance intra-organizational communication. — Filters reports and data and forwards to appropriate executives.	— Reads reports and pertinent professional literature. — Sets policy that impacts intra-organizational communications.
Communication (Inter-organizational)		— Attends professional meetings and conferences.	— Attends professional meetings and conferences. — Meets with key visitors.	— Attends professional meetings and conferences. — Meets with key visitors. — Liaisons with other organizations and companies.
Performance Management	— Orients new employee to specific job in work unit. — Provides information for job description.	— Orients new employee to specific job in work unit. — Creates job descriptions.	— Orients new employee to specific job in work unit.	

(continued)

ORGANIZATIONAL LEADERSHIP ASSESSMENT (continued)

Performance Management (continued)	Supervisor	Middle Manager	Top-Level Manager	Executive
	— Participates in interviewing candidates.	— Sets up system for obtaining pool of candidates	— Conducts job interviews.	— Conducts job interviews.
	— Organizes the work for employees.	— Formulates procedures for organizing work.		
	— Organizes necessary equipment, supplies, and job aids.		— Allocates resources for equipment and supplies.	— Sets policy.
	— Works closely with employees and monitors performance daily.	— Reviews performance evaluations and communicates with top management.		
		— Establishes performance-review procedures and reporting process.		
		— Provides training in performance management.	— Establishes policies and resources for performance-management programs.	
	— Regularly recognizes individual and team performance.	— Establish recognition programs.	— Establishes policy and resources to ensure recognition of performance.	— Establishes policy and resources to ensure recognition of performance.

	Column 1	Column 2	Column 3	Column 4
	— Participates in and creates own team celebrations. — Participates in development programs. — Recommends employees for advancement.	— Researches and recommends ways to celebrate accomplishments and progress. — Establishes programs for development, succession planning, and advancement. — Recommends employees for advancement.	— Participates in and creates own team celebrations. — Ensures allocation of resources for development, succession planning, and advancement. — Recommends employees for advancement.	— Leads the organization's celebrations. — Establishes policy for development, succession planning, and advancement.
Coaching and Counseling	— Assesses and recommends employees for appropriate career-development opportunities.	— Researches career-development techniques, tools, and programs. — Recommends and implements approved programs. — Selects career-assessment tools and techniques. — Provides training in career coaching.	— Finds resources for career coaching and development. — Approves programs.	— Establishes policy for Career Coaching.

(continued)

ORGANIZATIONAL LEADERSHIP ASSESSMENT (continued)

	Supervisor	Middle Manager	Top-Level Manager	Executive
Coaching and Counseling (continued)	— Coaches troubled employees. — Refers employees to Employee Assistance.	— Provides coaching and training for troubled employees. — Establishes Employee Assistance Programs.	— Allocates resources for Employee Assistance Programs.	— Sets policy for Counseling.
Human Relations (Intra-group)	— Is aware of own attitudes, assumptions, and beliefs about people. — Develops a work environment that is supportive and that involves other people. — Shows continual interest in employee needs and problems, and responds appropriately. — Facilitates resolution of conflict in own work unit.	— Establishes programs to foster appreciation of others' values, attitudes, and beliefs. — Applies knowledge of group dynamics and human behavior to all programs. — Shows continual interest in employee needs and problems, and responds appropriately. — Resolves difficult inter-personal and inter-unit conflicts.	— Develops policy endorsing diversity of personnel. — Works to create supportive work culture. — Shows continual interest in employee needs and problems, and responds appropriately. — Resolves difficult inter-personal and inter-unit conflicts.	— Develops policy endorsing diversity of personnel. — Sets the tone of the organization's culture. — Shows continual interest in employee needs and problems, and responds appropriately. — Resolves difficult inter-personal and inter-unit conflicts.

Human Relations (Inter-group)	— Interprets and applies goals of organization to work unit. — Reports employee needs to middle management.	— Establishes programs to facilitate the implementation of goals of organization. — Integrates employee needs into plans for organization.	— Establishes goals for inter-group relations. — Develops policies that integrate various employee needs.	— Develops policy for inter-group relations. — Develops policies that integrate various employee needs. — Represents organization with outside groups.
Decision-Making	— Makes concrete, pragmatic, and daily decisions that impact work unit. — Makes short-term decisions. — Uses appropriate decision-making processes. — Seeks advice from above regarding difficult decisions. — Carries out decisions from above.	— Makes decisions that are practical applications of abstract and strategic organizational issues and problems. — Reviews implications of long-term decisions. — Selects appropriate decision-making processes, and provides training. — Seeks advice from above regarding difficult decisions. — Carries out decisions from above.	— Makes abstract and strategic organizational decisions. — Makes long-term decisions. — Provides guidance regarding difficult decisions.	— Makes abstract and strategic organizational decisions. — Makes long-term decisions. — Establishes effective decision-making climate. — Provides guidance regarding difficult decisions. — Is accountable for organizational decisions.

(continued)

ORGANIZATIONAL LEADERSHIP ASSESSMENT (continued)

	Supervisor	Middle Manager	Top-Level Manager	Executive
Decision-Making (continued)		___ Assesses economic, social, and political factors related to organization's needs, survival, and future.	___ Reviews assessments of economic, social, and political factors related to organization's needs, survival, and future.	___ Reviews assessments of economic, social, and political factors related to organization's needs, survival, and future.
Planning	___ Participates in establishing the organization's vision. ___ Provides work unit action plans. ___ Assigns work and schedules according to plan. ___ Takes short-term risks after careful analysis. ___ Identifies fiscal needs.	___ Participates in establishing the organization's vision. ___ Develops action plans. ___ Establishes procedures for implementing work plans. ___ Integrates budget needs from all units.	___ Participates in establishing the organization's vision. ___ Allocates resources for implementing plans.	___ Uses assessments to forecast the organization's future. ___ Establishes organization's vision and direction with strategic goals. ___ Approves action plans. ___ Reviews results. ___ Takes long-term risks after careful analysis. ___ Approves budget.

A Plan for Leadership Development

DIRECTIONS: After assessing your skills in all six dimensions of leadership, enter up to three in each competency category below. Do not be concerned if you only have one skill to list in a particular dimension. If you have more than three that you want to develop, select the three that are most important for job success. We will be identifying strategies and resources that will help you to succeed.

SKILLS   STRATEGIES   RESOURCES

Communication
1. _____
2. _____
3. _____

1. _____
2. _____
3. _____

1. _____
2. _____
3. _____

Performance Management
1. _____
2. _____
3. _____

1. _____
2. _____
3. _____

1. _____
2. _____
3. _____

Coaching and Counseling
1. _____
2. _____
3. _____

1. _____
2. _____
3. _____

1. _____
2. _____
3. _____

Human Relations
1. _____
2. _____
3. _____

1. _____
2. _____
3. _____

1. _____
2. _____
3. _____

Decision-Making
1. _____
2. _____
3. _____

1. _____
2. _____
3. _____

1. _____
2. _____
3. _____

Planning
1. _____
2. _____
3. _____

1. _____
2. _____
3. _____

1. _____
2. _____
3. _____

18

THE LEADERSHIP CHALLENGE
The Kouzes-Posner Leadership Model

Overview of Activity

Kouzes and Posner (K & P) wrote a preface to the *Leadership Training Activity Book*. In this activity, the K&P 360 feedback instrument is utilized to identify a leader's strengths and those issues that require further exploration.

Objectives

→ To provide an overview of the Kouzes and Posner (KP) leadership model.

→ To explain how the *Leadership Practices Inventory* is interpreted and used in professional development.

→ To show how this assessment should be integrated into the leadership program you are conducting.

→ To use the IDEA team process (outlined in Activity 2).

Setting Up the Activity

GROUP SIZE
A maximum of 20 participants

ESTIMATED TIME
→ 1 hour for pre-workshop assignment
→ 2 hours for workshop

TRAINING METHODS
→ Self-Assessment
→ Presentation
→ Discussion
→ Feedback
→ Reflection
→ Writing

MATERIALS

The Leadership Challenge, by James Kouzes and Barry Posner (3rd Edition) San Francisco: Jossey Bass, 2002

Leadership Practices Inventory: Self and *LPI-Others Leadership Practices Inventory* created by Kouzes, Jim and Barry Posner is available in paper and on-line formats (2004). Visit www.lpionline.com

Handout 18.1: *The Kouzes and Posner Five Practices of Exemplary Leadership®**

EQUIPMENT AND SUPPLIES
Overhead projector for transparencies

ROOM SET-UP
Tables and chairs

Comments

We used the work of James Kouzes and Barry Posner as the framework for our leadership program, and we recommend that you do the same. You will need to read their book *The Leadership Challenge (third edition)* and refer to the trainers' manual for the *Leadership Practices Inventory.* Kouzes and Posner use the word "practices" to describe a category of leadership skills or competencies.

This activity is designed to use the IDEA teams discussed in Activity 2. We suggest that you use two other activities that complement the Kouzes and Posner model from Lois Hart's *50 Activities for Developing Leaders: Volume I* (HRD Press, 1994).

The first activity we suggest is *Common Themes in Leadership Research.* Its purpose is to provide the context for the Kouzes and Posner model. Research on leadership competencies continues to validate the five competencies first outlined by Kouzes and Posner, including much material published since Lois Hart completed Volume 1 of this

---

*The Five Practices of Exemplary Leadership® is a registered trademark of James M. Kouzes and Barry Z. Posner.

book. You can add or substitute any of these new works and still facilitate this important discussion.

The second activity we hope you incorporate is *Leading at Your Best*. Kouzes and Posner conducted their original research by querying people about those times when they knew they were doing their best leading. This activity from Volume I of this book is an adaptation of their original set of questions. If you use *Leading at Your Best* before introducing the Kouzes and Posner model here, participants will be able to practice storytelling.

The third activity we recommend is *Writing a Professional Development Plan*. Apply it as presented or create a planning activity of your own. We believe that getting participants to create their own written plans is a critical element of every leader's work. How can you get where you're going if you don't have a guide to help you along the way?

Resources

The Kouzes and Posner books, training manual, and instruments are available through Jossey Bass/Pfeiffer (a Wiley company). Contact Wiley at 1-800-956-7739.

Trainer's Notes for Activity 18

ADVANCE PREPARATION

Distribute this self-assessment of leadership skills a day or so before you plan to distribute the results. Tell each participant to complete the *Leadership Practices Inventory: Self*. Ask them to distribute the *Leadership Practices Inventory: Others* to his or her manager and four others who report to him or her, or to colleagues who have observed the individual's leadership behaviors.

STEP-BY-STEP PROCEDURE

Step 1: Present the Kouzes-Posner model, and explain the benefits of feedback. Have participants go over the review of the KP model as presented in the training manual and discuss how the data will be helpful. Review components of the feedback report, first using a hypothetical example. Refer to the LPI Trainer's Manual for this, because each step is outlined in the participant's notebook. Then review the guidelines (in the LPI Trainer's Manual) for giving feedback and helping others evaluate the information received in the feedback.

Step 2: Assess the information from the *Leadership Practices Inventory.* Have the IDEA teams sit at different tables, each with a facilitator. Distribute the results of the *Leadership Practices Inventory* to participants, using the steps outlined in the training manual. Reassure them by explaining

- who sees the data.
- how they should share data with others.
- how this assessment will contribute to their leadership development.

Step 3: This next assignment will be done individually. Distribute Handout 18.1. Ask participants to sit someplace quiet. Give them *one hour* to identify their personal strengths, as well as areas that could stand some improvement. Direct them to write down specific goals and action. Explain the steps for creating a professional-development plan:

a. After participants study their reports, ask them to focus on one of five competencies. Tell them to use the form provided to write out the goal and learning activities.

b. Next, give individuals time to study the data and highlight those areas they intend to work on at a later time. They do not need to write out all the details at this point because they will do this with their coach.

Step 4: This next segment is all about the professional development process. At the end of the hour, ask participants to reassemble into their IDEA teams. The facilitator should go over the professional development planning process to be used in your leadership program and answer any questions. Review steps for developing a plan, and distribute the forms.

Give each person a chance to share his or her primary goal with the rest of the IDEA team, along with a few details. No advice is given at this point.

Step 5: Discuss why it is important to share one's goals with the manager and staff. Review how to do this (refer to the LPI Trainer's Manual).

Step 6: Summary: The information you have gotten from this instrument will be helpful to you throughout the remainder of this leadership program. When we present a leadership skill that is related to the Kouzes and Posner model, we will ask you to look back at the appropriate data in your report.

POST-ACTIVITY REVIEW

Take time shortly after conducting this activity to reflect on how it went, how engaged the participants were, and what questions they raised. Then, make notes that include how much time you actually spent on the activity.

The Kouzes and Posner Five Practices of Exemplary Leadership*

1. Model the way.

→ Do what you say you are going to do.

→ Have a discussion on personal and shared values.

→ Measure the important things. What gets measured gets done.

→ Trade places with others in other areas for a day.

→ Be willing to do some of the hard things you ask others to do.

→ Make a plan, so that large projects are broken into small wins.

2. Inspire a shared vision.

→ Be clear about the strengths of the past.

→ Be aware of the values and motivations of those with whom you work.

→ Construct a vision statement, and have others add their feedback.

→ Keep your eye on the big picture, and keep heading on that path.

→ Speak positively.

→ Listen first and often.

3. Challenge the process.

→ Question the status quo.

→ Find something that needs fixing.

→ Add adventure and challenge to the work process.

*The Five Practices of Exemplary Leadership® is a registered trademark of James M. Kouzes and Barry Z. Posner.

EXEMPLARY LEADERSHIP (continued)

→ Be open to new ideas.

→ Model risk-taking.

→ Debrief every failure as well as every success.

→ Be open to feedback coming from other industries, departments, customers, and vendors.

4. Enable others to act.

→ Be inclusive. Use "we" instead of "I" whenever possible.

→ Increase connections with the people you work with.

→ Collaborate with others to plan or solve problems.

→ Share information instead of hoarding it.

→ Focus on gains, not losses.

→ Give power and opportunity to others.

→ Enlarge everyone's sphere of influence.

→ Educate, educate, educate.

5. Encourage the heart.

→ Celebrate successes with creative rewards and personal recognition.

→ Find out what will be rewarding to members of your team.

→ Catch people doing things right and give them immediate feedback.

→ Coach others by being clear about strengths and weaknesses.

→ Find ways to make work more fun.

Take time to build your own professional and social network.

19

SORT OUT
MANAGER-VS.-LEADER
COMPETENCIES

Overview of Activity

A manager brings many positive attributes to the new role of leader. There are some competencies that the manager must leave behind when assuming the leadership role. This card sort helps the participants think through this important growth process.

Objectives

→ To clarify the difference between the role of a manager and the role of a leader.

→ To identify which behaviors are still appropriate or expected as an individual moves from one role to another.

→ To define which tasks and responsibilities can be passed to others as one moves from a manager to a leader.

→ To encourage participants to think through which key competencies they still have to attain as they shift from manager to leader.

→ To celebrate the skills individuals have developed or improved as manager or as leader.

Setting Up the Activity

GROUP SIZE
Maximum of 10 participants per facilitator

ESTIMATED TIME
1 to 1¼ hours

TRAINING METHODS
➜ Discussion (in pairs and in a large group)
➜ Card-sort activity
➜ Reflection

MATERIALS
A deck of cards for each person, on which are written the competencies shown on Job Aid 19.1: *Manager vs. Leader Competencies.*

EQUIPMENT AND SUPPLIES
➜ Two flipcharts
➜ Markers
➜ Stick-on dots and stars
➜ Paper and pen/pencil for each person

ROOM SET-UP
Enough open space for participants to spread out their cards on the floor.

Comments

Many theorists have done extensive research on the differences between leaders and managers. In his book *A Force for Change,* John Kotter clearly outlines those differences. Generally, he says, those differences look something like this:

	A Manager . . .	**A Leader . . .**
To create an agenda	Plans steps, timelines, budgets, and resources.	Establishes direction and vision.
To develop a human network for achieving the agenda	Organizes structure and staff, and establishes procedures to monitor implementation.	Aligns people behind the vision.
To execute a plan	Minimizes deviations from plan to help produce predictable results.	Energizes people to overcome major obstacles toward achieving the vision.

This activity provides a hands-on way for participants to focus on their competencies and strengths, as well as identify areas that can be improved.

Trainer's Notes for Activity 19

STEP-BY-STEP PROCEDURE

Step 1: Divide participants into pairs. Ask each person to identify several competencies they believe leaders must have and competencies that are necessary for managers. Take notes. [15 minutes]

Step 2: Reassemble and share the findings with the entire group. List the competencies on two separate flipchart sheets (one for leaders and one for managers). [10 minutes]

Step 3: Pass out one deck of cards for each pair of participants (but have enough for each person, so that when the exercise is completed, each person can leave with one deck). Ask each pair to spread the cards on the floor in two columns: one for leadership competencies and one for manager competencies. Participants may add new competencies that are not in the deck or eliminate any that do not seem to fit either category. Have blank cards ready for this. [10 minutes]

Step 4: Compare lists when every pair has finished. Ask everyone to move around to see what choices others have made. [5 minutes]

Step 5: Compare Manager competencies and Leader competencies by posting these questions on the flipchart and discussing participant responses:

– What manager competencies do we agree on?

– What leadership competencies do we agree on?

– What are the competencies you respect most in the leaders with whom you work?

Step 6: Pass out the handout *Manager vs. Leader Competencies* and a sheet of small stick-on stars. Ask participants to read the handout and place a star on the items they feel they ready do well. Ask them to use the small dots to mark 3 to 5 areas that they want to focus on as part of their professional development. [7–10 minutes]

Step 7: Summarize and bring the activity to a close. Pose these questions for discussion:

→ What holds back a manager from becoming a leader?

→ What do you think your greatest challenge will be as you make the transition?

POST-ACTIVITY REVIEW

Take time shortly after conducting this activity to reflect on how it went, how engaged the participants were, and what questions they raised. Then, make notes that include how much time you actually spent on the activity.

Manager vs. Leader Competencies

A MANAGER	A LEADER
Has a short-range perspective.	Has a long-range perspective.
Plans *how* and *when.*	Asks *what* and *why.*
Eyes the bottom line.	Eyes the horizon.
Imitates others.	Originates.
Accepts the status quo.	Challenges the status quo.
Does things correctly.	Does the correct thing.
Seeks continuity.	Seeks change.
Focuses on goals for improvement.	Focuses on goals of innovation.
Power is based on position or authority.	Power is based on personal influence.
Demonstrates skill in technical competence.	Demonstrates skill in selling the vision.
Demonstrates skill in administration.	Demonstrates skill in dealing with ambiguity.
Demonstrates skill in supervision.	Demonstrates skill in persuasion.
Works toward employee compliance.	Works toward employee commitment.
Plans tactics.	Plans strategy.
Sets standard operating procedures.	Sets policy.
Relies on analytical decision-making style.	Relies on intuitive decision-making style.
Is risk cautious.	Takes the necessary risks.
Uses a "transactional" communication style.	Uses a "transformational" communication style.
Mostly uses an informational base of data and facts.	Uses an informational base, including "gut" feelings.
Builds success through maintenance of quality.	Builds success through employee commitment.
Does not want to experience anarchy.	Does not want to experience inertia.
Plans, budgets, and designs detail steps.	Develops the vision and the strategies to achieve it.
Sets standards of performance.	Sets standards of excellence.
Develops the detailed plan to achieve results.	Develops the future direction by gathering future trends.

20

LEAD THEM
ON AN ADVENTURE!

Overview of Activity

A brief hike is used as a metaphor for leaders with flexibility and an adventuresome spirit. Hikers (participants) carry backpacks full of typical items needed for a such a walk and relate them to specific leadership competencies.

Objectives

➔ To identify one's willingness to be flexible, adventuresome, and interested in trying something new.

➔ To confirm that taking the initiative is an essential skill possessed by all effective leaders.

Setting Up the Activity

GROUP SIZE
Maximum of 10 participants per facilitator

ESTIMATED TIME
1 hour

TRAINING METHODS
➔ Movement
➔ Discussion

MATERIALS
None

EQUIPMENT AND SUPPLIES

→ Large backpacks or travel bags that can hold the other items
→ Day backpacks
→ Hiking boots
→ Binoculars
→ Outdoor hats

→ Water bottles
→ Blankets
→ Trail food
→ Maps
→ Compass

ROOM SET-UP
Select a place outdoors where you can take your participants on a 10-minute walk and then sit for the discussion.

Trainer's Notes for Activity 20

STEP-BY-STEP PROCEDURE

Step 1: Tell participants that leaders must demonstrate an adventuresome spirit. They must be flexible and innovative and take appropriate risks, so their followers can learn from them.

Step 2: Gather participants around the backpack or duffel bag full of supplies for the upcoming walk. Explain that you are going on an adventure outside. Pull out the supplies and assign different people to carry them as you build up excitement. Instruct them to get their coats and prepare for an adventure. Ask them to pick a walking partner.

Step 3: As you lead them to your destination, ask the walking partners to tell one another about a time they embarked on a great travel or hiking adventure, particularly one that was different from what they would normally do or different from where they usually travel or hike.

Step 4: When everyone arrives at the destination, spread out the blankets, get out the snacks and water bottles, and make everyone comfortable. Together, discuss their personal adventures, asking questions such as these:

→ What do you especially remember about how your earlier adventure made you feel?

→ What did you learn after taking these adventures?

➔ Tell about a time in your work when you made a radical departure from the way you usually do things—a time when you were adventuresome.

➔ What are the common elements found in these stories?

➔ In the adventure we just shared, how did the element of suspense about where we were going affect you?

➔ What do binoculars have to do with a work adventure?

➔ What are the important supplies we should have on hand as we plan an adventure?

Step 5: Relate the discussion you've just had to leadership. Tell participants that research shows that effective leaders are adventuresome in spirit and are willing to go in new directions. They experiment, take risks, and challenge systems to create new products, processes, and services. These leaders learn from the inevitable mistakes that occur when risks are taken. Say:

"Leaders differ from managers when they face change and risks. Effective leaders evaluate their propensity toward taking risks, analyze whether the risks they have taken in the past were appropriate, and know that the ability to take measured risks is a leadership skill. Leaders are willing to take those risks once they are fully prepared for the consequences."

Step 6: Bring the session to a close by asking participants: what have you learned that can applied to your role as a leader?

POST-ACTIVITY REVIEW

Take time shortly after conducting this activity to reflect on how it went, how engaged the participants were, and what questions they raised. Then, make notes that include how much time you actually spent on the activity.

21

TRUST
The Glue of Leadership

Overview of Activity

Using a blindfold, one participant allows another to walk about, while using only non-verbal clues. The debriefing takes each of the partners in the exercise through communication, trust, and other issues that leaders face.

Objectives

→ To develop trust among program participants (this will make their experiences mutually rewarding).

→ To help participants experience the meaning of "leader" versus "follower."

→ To learn the value of nonverbal communication.

Setting Up the Activity

GROUP SIZE
Any size group, but an even number of participants works best because of paired exercises

ESTIMATED TIME
30 to 60 minutes

TRAINING METHODS

➔ Movement

➔ Discussion

➔ Reflection

MATERIALS

None

EQUIPMENT AND SUPPLIES

One blindfold per pair of participants (cloth strips)

ROOM SET-UP

A safe, open area

Comments

Use this activity only if you have an environment that is safe for conducting this activity, which involves a walk while blindfolded. Use it only with people who will respond well and learn from it. If anyone indicates he/she is uncomfortable doing this, be sure to respect their wishes.

Trainer's Notes for Activity 21

STEP-BY-STEP PROCEDURE

Step 1: Introduce the topic by explaining the importance of building trust among those we lead. Refer to the dynamics and activities of professional workshops (including this one), where colleagues and often complete strangers share ideas and experiences to derive the most benefit from the program.

Step 2: Divide participants into two equal groups. Have one group stand and the other sit. Instruct those seated to close their eyes. Ask those who are standing to silently walk around and mentally select a seated partner. They should then stand behind that person's chair and tie a blindfold on him or her without revealing their identity or giving clues.

Step 3: Explain that the "sighted" partners will guide their blindfolded partners on a 5-minute walk using only nonverbal directions. The guides must use the entire environment (rooms, hallways, stairs, and outdoors), but they must always consider their partner's safety and willingness to try a new experience.

Allow only 5 minutes for the walk-about. After 4 minutes, give a 1-minute warning.

Step 4: When everyone has returned, allow the "blind" participants to remove their blindfolds to see who guided them. Then have the pairs compare their experiences using these questions:

→ For *blindfolded* partners:
- Did you have any idea of your leader's identity?
- What did your leader do that made your walk easy or difficult?
- How do you feel toward your partner now?

→ For *sighted* partners:
- What made this task difficult for you?
- How did you plan your walk?
- How do you feel toward your partner now?

Step 5: Reassemble and compare notes on the experience, focusing on the importance of trust.

Step 6: Reverse the roles, but change partners so that the blindfolded partner is led by someone new. Explain that this second round gives the new leaders a chance to apply what they learned while being led. After the 5-minute walk, have partners discuss the questions in Step 3.

Step 7: Lead a summary discussion with the total group. Review the experience itself and relate it to the content of your workshop. Ask these questions of the group, and allow volunteers to respond:

- How can the trust walks enhance our remaining time together?

- How can you improve the way you communicate, from now on?

- What did this teach you about the role of a follower, versus the role of a leader?

POST-ACTIVITY REVIEW

Take time shortly after conducting this activity to reflect on how it went, how engaged the participants were, and what questions they raised. Then, make notes that include how much time you actually spent on the activity.

22

A METAPHOR FOR PERSONAL CHANGE

From Caterpillars to Butterflies

Overview of Activity

Personal change is an essential underpinning of leadership development. This exercise takes participants through a series of discrete steps that will occur as part of the change process

Objectives

→ To provide a framework for thinking about change as a critical element in your corporate and personal lives.

→ To demonstrate how to use metaphors as part of your thinking process.

→ To gather participant ideas regarding change.

→ To offer options regarding the stages of change.

→ To identify what change stage each participant is currently in as he/she shares a personal change.

→ To understand that risk is part of change.

Setting Up the Activity

GROUP SIZE

10 to 20 participants is the best number, but the size of the room (see below) will in part dictate the number of participants, as they need to move about easily.

ESTIMATED TIME

1½ hours. If you have more time, don't limit the questions and discussions. This activity can easily be a two-hour module.

TRAINING METHODS

→ Discussion   → Movement

→ Storytelling   → Metaphor

→ Reflection   → Presentation

MATERIALS

→ Signs that denote the Stages of Change (see list in Step 3)

→ Diagram of the stages of change

→ Toy caterpillars and butterflies

EQUIPMENT AND SUPPLIES

→ Two flipcharts on easels. One should have a prepared list of answers for the caterpillar/butterfly paradox referred to in Step 2.

→ Markers

→ Masking tape and scotch tape

→ Balloons (long shape, to mimic caterpillars)

→ Ball of yarn that gets pulled apart on the floor to make the Stages-of-Change shape

→ Index cards

ROOM SET-UP

The room has to be large enough to accommodate the large Stages-of-Change shape created from the yarn. Participants can sit wherever they wish at the sides of the room. They will be getting up later.

Comments

This engaging and lively exercise should be used when you want participants to get up and move around. Try to use it before everyone has to begin adjusting to a dramatic change (downsizing, restructuring, mergers, acquisitions, relocation, or any other major corporate change that will affect people who must continue to work in the midst of turmoil or uncertainty). Refer to Activity 44 on Risk for complementary exercises. Before you begin the module, hang butterflies on the wall and drape the yarn into the appropriate shape.

VARIATIONS

John L. Bennett, in his article in the September 2001 issue of *HR Magazine,* identified a number of things leaders can do to deal with change. Consider using these prepared suggestions, especially if your group is not a talkative one. Put each suggestion on an index card, and ask each participant to pick one and talk about it.

→ Admit that many changes cannot be controlled; they are imposed upon us. Talk about one of these changes.

→ Identify those things, events, emotions, and responses that you can control, as opposed to what you can only influence. What might some appropriate actions be?

→ Seek to understand the change being implemented and your response to it before you attempt to have others understand you and your response. Describe a time when you used this strategy.

→ Develop or strengthen your network of support for embracing the change. Which people are most likely to help you embrace the change?

→ Increase your conscious attention to maintaining a balanced, healthy lifestyle: mental, emotional, physical, and spiritual. Where are you planning to begin?

→ Seek to understand the origin of your fears, anger, and resentments about the change. Discuss one of the issues you face.

→ Consciously develop a plan to overcome the causes of resistance to change and build on your strengths. Don't focus on your disappointment and weaknesses. Where might you begin?

→ Look for the positive benefits of embracing the change, rather than dwell on the past or any negative implications you perceive. Share an example.

→ Realize that change is likely to occur, whether or not you embrace it. What is one positive thing you can do?

REFERENCES

Bennett, John L. "Change Happens." *HR Magazine* 42 (September 2001): 148–156.

Bridges, William. Managing Transitions: Making the Most of Change. Reading MA: Addision Wesley, 1991.

Kubler-Ross, Elisabeth. On Death and Dying. NY: Schribner Book Co., 1997.

Trainer's Notes for Activity 22

STEP-BY-STEP PROCEDURE

Step 1: Introduce the topic of personal change by asking:

➜ "When I say the word CHANGE, what comes to mind?" (Record answers on the flipchart.)

➜ "Is it helpful to divide change into personal change and professional change? Why or why not?"

➜ "You might notice some butterflies around the room. Any ideas as to why they are posted?"

➜ "Here's a balloon for you. Please blow it up and tie it." (See if anyone makes a connection between the caterpillar and the butterfly as you show some tiny caterpillar toys.)

➜ "Yes, caterpillars evolve into butterflies. Have you ever seen it happen?"

Step 2: Tell the following story and lead a discussion about its meaning:

"Two caterpillars, sitting on the leaves of a tree, are talking. A beautiful butterfly floats by. One caterpillar turns to the other and says, "You'll never get **me** up on one of those butterfly things."

Ask participants to consider the meaning of this story and look for some important perspectives. Elicit responses and put them on one of the flipcharts. Repeat the story if that helps to get more responses. Then say, "When I ask people to discuss the meaning of the story, I receive many different responses, including the ones on this flipchart." Show the one or two sheets on the flipchart with these ideas:

➜ Caterpillars have no need to fly. They are already well grounded!

➜ Caterpillars can eat anything green, and they find food everywhere.

➜ Butterflies are a stage beyond caterpillars.

➜ Butterflies have to fly to get anywhere. Caterpillars can crawl and climb.

➜ It's easier for butterflies to develop perspective than it is for caterpillars.

→ We can attempt to resist, but we will suffer stress and difficulty.

→ You have to stop being a caterpillar in order to become a butterfly.

→ Change is not always a conscious decision. Change will occur, inevitably.

→ We can choose to be active participants in change. (*Or not, maybe.*)

→ We go through stages of development, and butterflies are one stage closer to death.

→ Risk avoidance is normal.

→ Change is often actively resisted.

→ Change is inevitable.

→ Caterpillars don't like wings.

→ Caterpillars must hate flying, since they don't try.

All of us have the capability to generate ideas and possibilities. Most of us would agree that being a butterfly is a "higher existence" than remaining a caterpillar. The story also links to some key learning points on change. Any ideas?"

Try to elicit the following ideas:

→ Although we often resist change and risk, it is inevitable!

→ Change will occur. We can choose to be active participants and go with the flow, or we can attempt to resist and suffer the stresses.

→ Each of us goes through many stages of development; it is a process that occurs repeatedly, over time.

→ Our possibilities are endless! Choosing to change is an important part of improvement.

"A while back, a man I know asked me, 'Do you know about caterpillars and butterflies?' I said that I did not.

"He then shared a great quote that makes a wonderful transition to the issue of personal and organizational change. He said, 'In the change from being a caterpillar to becoming a butterfly, you're nothing more than a yellow, gooey sticky mess.'"

"We need to deal with the gooey glop that most people find uncomfortable. But you have to metamorphose in order to change, and that will involve going through the discomfort of being less and less a caterpillar while you are in the process of becoming a butterfly."

"Expect the transformation process to be somewhat uncomfortable. And it certainly requires some degree of risk!"

"A colleague explained it to me far more simply. She said, 'Change is a moment. Transition is the process. It is coming to terms with transition that takes our time and energy.'"

Step 3: Introduce a change model. Tell participants, "I'd like to focus now on personal change. Personal change is often a response to crisis. A number of theorists have written about this, but William Bridges comes to mind first. Has anyone read his work? He says that it is our responses—our reactions and our emotions—that make the transition of change so difficult.

"On the floor, you can see a modified 'grief' cycle depicted with yarn. Many theorists suggest that our response to change goes through stages that are much like the stages of death and dying that Elizabeth Kubler-Ross first wrote about.

"Even if you haven't read her work, those of you who are working together will understand it after this exercise. Take a few minutes to put the signs around the room in the order you believe represents the progressive cycle of change—the way you believe is real."

Direct the group's attention to the signs sitting on the side. They are NOT in order. Ask people to arrange them in order. Unless they are drastically wrong, don't correct the order of how they arranged the stages. It is the process of doing it together that is the focus.

(The correct order is **Crisis, Shock, Denial, Anger, Bargaining, Guilt, Panic, Depression, Resignation to Situation, Acceptance of Reality, Building,** and **Opportunity: Growth and New Directions**)

Step 4: Ask everyone to sit. Say, "Using the index card I hand you, take a few minutes to record three personal changes that you are currently experiencing. Then choose one that you are willing to share." Allow time to do this.

Step 5: Then say, "Get up, walk around, and stand near the sign that best describes the stage of change that you are currently in for a particular situation. Be prepared to discuss it with a partner. Now pair up." Then tell them in pairs to answer these questions:

→ Was this change thrust upon you? Is it clear where you are headed?

→ How are you letting go of where you were?

→ What happens when you let go of one moment, before you get to the next stage?

→ What risks did you take to make that change happen?

→ What will take you to the next stage?

→ Do you have the competencies and skills to get to the next stage?

→ What do you need to move on?

Allow time to do this.

Step 6: Debrief with the whole group, but try to get the quieter people to go first.

Step 7: Close the module by asking, "How can you as leader use concrete knowledge about personal change? Do you have all of the competencies you need to survive corporate change?" Discuss these questions together.

Step 8: Encourage people to write in their journals or notebooks about how they are weathering a change—a change talked about today, or a change with which they are currently coping.

POST-ACTIVITY REVIEW

Take time shortly after conducting this activity to reflect on how it went, how engaged the participants were, and what questions they raised. Then, make notes that include how much time you actually spent on the activity.

23

VALUES

The Foundation of Ethics

Overview of Activity

Leaders have responsibilities to themselves and to their organization to demonstrate their values at all times. This activity helps participants think through their standards.

Objectives

→ To help participants reaffirm their key values.

→ To identify how values become the foundation of our ethical standards, behavior, and decision-making.

Setting Up the Activity

GROUP SIZE
Up to 20 participants

ESTIMATED TIME
30 minutes

TRAINING METHODS
→ Reflection
→ Discussion

MATERIALS
None

EQUIPMENT AND SUPPLIES
12" × 17" paper and card stock

ROOM SET-UP
Enough tables and chairs for small groups

Comments

Our values become the foundation for our standards, decisions, and behavior as leaders. Therefore, this activity can be conducted before using Activity #23—Steps to Making Ethical Decisions.

RESOURCE
Dalke, David, and Anderstar, Sheryl. Balancing Personal and Professional Ethics. Amherst MA: HRD Press, 1995.

Trainer's Notes for Activity 23

STEP-BY-STEP PROCEDURE

Step 1: Introduce the topic and provide an overview. Say, "Values provide the foundation for our standards, decisions , and behavior as leaders. In this activity, you will identify several values that form the basis of who you are as an individual. Then we'll look at how your leadership values impact other people."

Step 2: Then define "value" as "a belief you hold so dearly, it permeates everything you do and say. Your belief is so strong that, when it is challenged, you do not hesitate to speak out and defend your position. We find that very few things fit this criteria at any one time, but the beliefs we hold are very dear."

Step 3: Ask participants to privately list ten values—tangible or intangible—that are extremely important to them—values that rule their lives.

Step 4: Divide participants into groups of four, and allow time for people to read their lists to one another. Ask people to share why they chose what they did.

Step 5: Then say, "Privately, take the list and draw a line through three values that are of lesser importance to you." When everyone is about finished, ask them to share what they eliminated with their groups.

Step 6: Next, say, "Now draw a line through three more values that are of lesser importance to you and write your top four values, one on each index card." Then have each person post their cards on a wall and see if anyone else shares their same values. Groups may move similar cards together to illustrate any commonality.

Step 7: Ask individuals if any of their values conflict with the values of their organizations. If so, have the participant take his or her card off the wall and explain how this discrepancy might be dealt with at work.

Step 8: Ask people to try one more round of elimination to select their highest value. "Put a big star on your card and sign your name on it. Then do your next-highest value." Chose a partner and talk about times when someone questioned this value or they had to defend it.

Step 9: Bring the activity to a close by asking volunteers to try to summarize how important certain values are to the way they handle their responsibilities to the organization and to themselves. How is the organization affected by the values of its employees?

POST-ACTIVITY REVIEW

Take time shortly after conducting this activity to reflect on how it went, how engaged the participants were, and what questions they raised. Then, make notes that include how much time you actually spent on the activity.

24

JUST DO THE RIGHT THING!
How to Make Ethical Decisions

Overview of Activity

The step-by-step process that clarifies how ethical decisions are made is demonstrated in this exercise.

Objectives

→ To present a way to thoroughly think things out before taking action.

→ To demonstrate how to clarify, explore, and examine all options to arrive at ethical decisions.

Setting Up the Activity

GROUP SIZE
Up to 20 participants

ESTIMATED TIME
1 hour

TRAINING METHODS
→ Storytelling
→ Reflection
→ Journal writing
→ Scenarios
→ Presentation

MATERIALS
Handout 24.1: *How to Make Ethical Decisions*

EQUIPMENT AND SUPPLIES
➔ Flipcharts and markers
➔ Large poster-size version of model

ROOM SET-UP
Arrange tables and chairs in a semicircle

Comments

Ask people to discuss ethical dilemmas with which they are familiar so the model can be applied to real-life situations. Send out a few assignments in advance, such as:

➔ Identify 3 to 5 personal standards you live by. (Review your list of values to help you.) Identify any written or unwritten standards your company lives by.

➔ Identify a time at work when you felt as if your ethical standards were threatened or compromised.

➔ Contact your trainer in advance if you are currently facing an ethical dilemma that you are willing to talk about in the workshop.

VARIATION
Instead of using examples from participants, write a case study or select one from a published source (such as the one here) to use for the activity.

RESOURCE
Dalke, David, and Anderstar, Sheryl. Balancing Personal and Professional Ethics. Amherst MA: HRD Press, 1995.

Trainer's Notes for Activity 24

STEP-BY-STEP PROCEDURE

Step 1: Introduce the topic by summarizing various highly publicized breaches of ethics (such as the Enron scandal) or an ethical dilemma you have personally faced. You could also invite a guest who tells an ethical story that will set the stage for this activity.

Step 2: Define "ethics" by asking participants to explain what the word means to them. List their answers on the flipchart. They are likely to mention beliefs, values, standards, and moral fiber. Write this formula on another piece of flipchart paper and post it:

Ethics = Character and concern for the community or the organization

Step 3: Say, "Ethics comes from the Greek word *ethos*—character, one's distinguishing attitudes and beliefs. Its secondary application is concern for the community or organization." Our ethos, our character, determines how we make decisions that affect not only us but also those around us: people in our community or place of work, our friends, and our family. We do not live in isolation; we live in a connected society.

All of our decisions, whether at work or in our personal lives, affect others. Therefore, we must consider this impact when we make decisions. Ethics means giving honest consideration to underlying motives and potential harm, if any, and to congruency with established values."

Step 4: Then say, "Now it's time to go over the steps we must take when making ethical decisions." Pass out Handout 24.1, and refer to a large poster-size version of the model. Go over each step with participants and use real-life examples of an ethical dilemma to explain the steps.

Step 5: Divide participants into groups of 3 to 5 people. One person at a time presents an ethical dilemma, while the other three discuss it by going through all of the steps of the model. With the total group, debrief how the process can help us resolve an ethical dilemma.

Step 6: Summarize this activity by going over the basics of the process, step by step. Sugggest that when they face their next ethical dilemma they review the handout and record their answers in their journals.

POST-ACTIVITY REVIEW

Take time shortly after conducting this activity to reflect on how it went, how engaged the participants were, and what questions they raised. Then, make notes that include how much time you actually spent on the activity.

How to Make Ethical Decisions

What is the ethical dilemma you are currently struggling with?

→ What doesn't feel right?

→ What feelings does it bring up for you?

→ What are the issues?

→ Why are these issues a concern of yours?

→ What are the facts around this dilemma?

What are your personal and organizational standards?

1. Personal Standards

→ Review your values.

→ How do you usually resolve conflicts?

2. Organizational Standards

→ What policies, practices, or written code of ethics exist in your organization?

→ What behaviors or decisions create your organizational standards?

Develop your preliminary decision, and conduct an analysis.

1. Motive

→ Why do you want to do something about this dilemma?

→ Why does the organization (or customers, employees, or stockholders) want to do this?

2. Process

→ What are optional ways to do this?

→ How will the method you are choosing help achieve the desired end?

HOW TO MAKE ETHICAL DECISIONS (continued)

➜ Is this process in alignment with your values?

➜ Is this process in alignment with your standards?

➜ Do you need more time to consider the best process or method to use?

➜ Is there anyone else who can provide input or counsel?

3. Consequences

➜ Will this decision violate any laws?

➜ Will this decision compromise any personal or organizational standards?

➜ How will this decision or action affect you in the long- and short-term?

➜ How will this decision or action affect others in the long- and short-term?

➜ Will this decision or action cause harm at any level?

Finalize your options. What are you willing to do?

➜ Act now—go ahead with the plan.

➜ Do nothing.

➜ Alter the plan of action.

Act on your decision.

25

I WANT SOME POWER!

Types of Power

Overview of Activity

This leadership competency is explored through brainstorming, working in dyads, and guided visualization.

Objectives

→ To define power.

→ To demonstrate the relationship between power and self–concept.

→ To identify positive and negative views we have of ourselves and how this impacts others.

→ To recognize that personal power comes from within.

→ To identify ways we give away power.

→ To identify ways to enhance personal power.

Setting Up the Activity

GROUP SIZE
Up to 20 participants

ESTIMATED TIME
1 hour

TRAINING METHODS

➔ Self-assessment

➔ Discussions

➔ Dyads

➔ Brainstorming

➔ Guided Visualization

MATERIALS

Handout 25.1: *Exploring My Personal Power*

Handout 25.2: *Sunshine and Clouds*

EQUIPMENT AND SUPPLIES

➔ Posters or pictures of some well-known people who represent power

➔ Flip charts and easels

➔ Colorful markers

ROOM SET-UP

Chairs and enough space to form dyads and reform for total group discussions.

Comments

Leaders have power, want power, use power and, hopefully, find ways to share power, give power and develop power in others. Power should not be viewed as a manipulative or "bad" aspect of leadership. Power and self-concept go hand in hand. Integrity with regard to the use of power is firmly based on a clear understanding of one's own power.

Trainer's Notes for Activity 25

STEP-BY-STEP PROCEDURE

Step 1: Put the word "Power" on the flipchart. Ask, "what is your definition of personal power, as used in a business context?" Write the participants' answers on the flipchart. Possible answers might include:

"Power is the ability to make and carry out decisions over time."

"Power is the ability to meet a need through access to and use of resources."

Step 2: Ask, "How do you feel about your own power?" Write "Power Means. . . ." on the flipchart. Elicit responses and write key words on the flipchart.

Step 3: Distribute the Handout 25.1, *Exploring My Personal Power,* and ask participants to complete it in approximately 10 minutes. Remind them to "be as honest and open as they can be in completing the questions. Also, to try to always think of business examples."

Step 4: Form dyads and ask them to share some of the insights from what they wrote on the handout. Allow a few to report back to the group as a whole.

Step 5: Ask them to look at the posters or pictures of famous leaders you have on the wall and then to stand by the one that represents a powerful person to them.

　　　Solicit reasons why they think these people are powerful. Write key responses on the flipchart.

Step 6: Ask, "Give me examples of a powerless person and explain your choice." Write key responses on the flipchart.

　　　Ask someone to volunteer to stand or sit like a powerless person would. Then, ask her or him to stay in that position and have the others comment.

Step 7: Then ask a second volunteer to stand or sit like a powerful person. While holding this stance, ask for comments. Some answers might include: The person acts confident. The body takes up 'space.' He or she stands firmly with both feet. The face may have controlled facial expression; alert but not highly emotional.

　　　Ask them to share the answer to this question in their same dyad. "Which type of person do you want to be and why?"

Step 8: Ask, "Do you know what your power is dependent upon?" Solicit some answers until someone suggests that one connection is self-concept. Distribute Handout 25.2, *Sunshine and Clouds.* Silently each person writes one to three beliefs that relate to personal power, beliefs that they hold about themselves for each of the following categories:

1. Intellectual
2. Physical
3. Emotional
4. Spiritual

When they are done, ask them to evaluate each belief:

"Is it positive? And if so, draw a sun next to it."

"Is it negative? And if so, draw a cloud next to it."

In dyads, ask them to discuss:

1. Are your beliefs about yourself mostly positive or negative?

2. How do the positive beliefs impact your use of personal power?

3. How do your negative beliefs impact your use of personal power?

In the total group, solicit sample answers to those three questions.

Step 9: Form two groups and have each stand by a piece of chart paper on the wall. Ask one person in each group to be the Recorder. Designate one group as the group that gives away power and the second group as the one that utilizes power appropriately. Ask each group to brainstorm for ten minutes and then offer examples that fit ways they either give away power or the ways they use power appropriately.

Step 10: Ask the group who identified ways we give away power to share their list and examples. Some ways might include:

→ Discount self.
→ Don't take responsibility.
→ Personal appearance.
→ Ways we stand.
→ Talk with quiet tone.
→ Nonassertive language.
→ Use of "I can't," "I should."
→ Limits one's options.
→ Fails to ask.
→ Procrastinates.
→ Doesn't plan carefully.
→ Failure to keep commitments.
→ Gestures like hand over mouth.
→ Cries publicly.
→ Yells and other rude behavior.

Step 11: Ask the group that identified ways we exercise power to share its list and examples. Some ways might include:

→ Believe in yourself.
→ Say what you want.
→ Use knowledge to back up what you say.
→ Be consistent.
→ Do what you say you'll do.
→ Accept responsibility.
→ Accept mistakes.
→ Remain open to options and alternative ideas.
→ Take risks.
→ Be good to yourself.
→ Don't avoid conflicts.
→ Plan.
→ Strategize before acting.
→ Trust your intuition.

Step 12: Ask participants to think about three ways they will utilize their personal power more. Ask them to write them on the bottom blank part of their *Exploring My Personal Power* handout.

Step 13: When they are done writing, lead them in a guided visualization. Do this slowly so they have time to imagine themselves.

"Get in a comfortable position and close your eyes. In your mind, see yourself on a stage in a large auditorium filled with people. You are a powerful person so I want you to say silently three times 'I am a powerful person'.

"What are your wearing and how are you standing?

"See yourself giving a presentation based on a topic where you have a lot of knowledge.

"How is the audience responding?

"How do you feel?

"Slowly open your eyes and look at all of the powerful people in this room."

Ask them to all stand up and give each other a "standing ovation!"

POST-ACTIVITY REVIEW

Take time shortly after conducting this activity to reflect on how it went, how engaged the participants were, and what questions they raised. Then, make notes that include how much time you actually spent on the activity.

Exploring My Personal Power

I feel my power when _____ ,
and I behave in the following ways:

I feel least powerful when _____ ,
and I react in the following ways:

I give away my power when _____ ,

and then I feel _____

I use my power appropriately when I _____ ,
and the results are:

I abuse my power when I _____ ,

and others reacted _____

Some sources of my power are:

Sunshine and Clouds

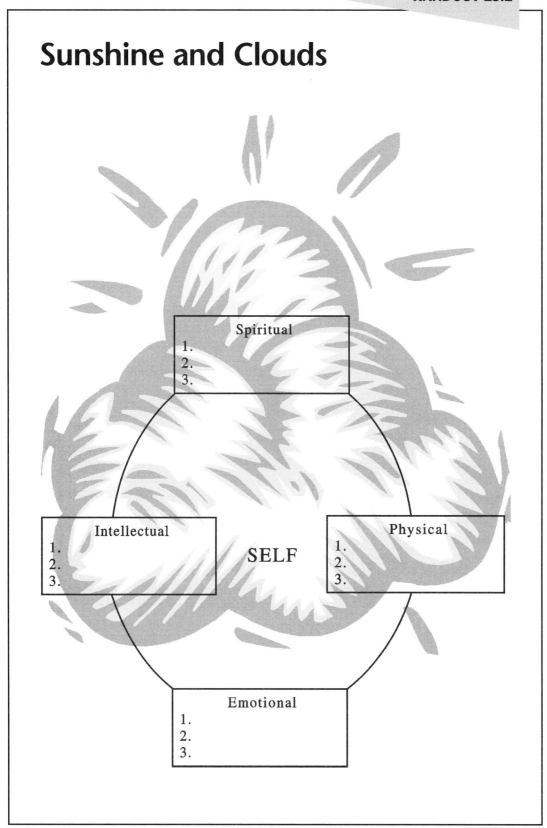

Spiritual
1.
2.
3.

Intellectual
1.
2.
3.

SELF

Physical
1.
2.
3.

Emotional
1.
2.
3.

26

YOU BE THE JUDGE!

Overview of Activity

A competitive game is used to identify various kinds of power.

Objectives

→ To develop the ability to identify and use different kinds of power.
→ To reinforce what has been learned about power.
→ To understand how others view power.

Setting Up the Activity

GROUP SIZE

20 participants is a comfortable size, but smaller numbers are fine

ESTIMATED TIME

45 minutes to 1 hour

TRAINING METHODS

→ Role Play
→ Game
→ Discussion

MATERIALS

→ Job Aid 26.1: *Scenario Descriptions* (the scenarios should be distributed one at a time)

→ Handout 26.1: *Types of Leadership Power*

→ One set of seven cards per group (a different kind of power from the sheet provided is printed on each card in letters large enough to be seen 15 feet away). See Job Aid 26.2: *Power Cards.*

EQUIPMENT AND SUPPLIES

→ Flipchart
→ Markers
→ One bell per small group
→ One judge's robe and wig (the "judge" can wear black clothes as an alternative)
→ Small prizes

Comments

Leaders derive power from their positions and personalities. In this activity, we practice exercising seven different kinds of power using a game with a courtroom setting. You will need one facilitator, and one person to be the judge. Dress the judge in black clothes or a judge's robe. Try to have a wig on hand for effect.

Consider awarding small prizes to the winners. This can be very energizing for competitive groups, as well as a rewarding way to build cohesive teams.

There is no one answer that fits each scenario. The dilemma can be "solved" in any number of ways. Sometimes more than one type of power is being used. (DO NOT share this information with the group until after the game has been played!)

After the groups identify the types of power used in the scenarios you provided, each group should write its own scenario and have the other groups guess which type of power is being used in the scenario.

Correct answers to each scenario in Job Aid 26.1

#1	Connection power	#5	Coercive power
#2	Information power	#6	Expert power
#3	Referent power	#7	Reward power
#4	Legitimate power		

Trainer's Notes for Activity 26

STEP-BY-STEP PROCEDURE

Step 1: Introduce the activity by asking, "What is your definition of *power* as it is used in your business context?" Elicit answers, and write them on the flipchart.

Then explain, "Communication is sometimes quite difficult, especially during the problem-solving process, when you are trying to understand another person's power base. It is always helpful to have a clear understanding of the underlying basis for the power you see demonstrated." (10 minutes)

Step 2: Discuss the seven general kinds of power (start by passing out Handout 26.1: *Types of Leadership Power*). The seven main types are:

1. "Coercive" power.
2. "Connection" power.
3. "Expert" power.
4. "Information" power.
5. "Legitimate" power.
6. "Referent" power.
7. "Reward" power.

Step 3: Tell the group that it's time to see how each type of power is used. Then begin playing the "You Be the Judge!" game.

1. Divide into groups of three-four and distribute one set of power cards to each group. Let each group pick a name for itself—the name of a famous leader. When the names have been chosen, write them in a list on the flipchart. The Judge will call the group by that name.

2. Explain the rules, as follows:

"You will be given a script of a short scenario in which the people involved exercise one type of power.

"After you read the scenario, talk among yourselves so the other groups can't hear, and decide what type of power is being demonstrated. Be sure you can defend the reasons why you make the choice you do and have that "power card" ready to show the Judge at the appropriate time.

"As soon as you have made a decision, ring the bell. In every round, we will record which group rang the bell first, but we will wait until every group has made a decision before the Judge hears them. You may use each power-type card only once. Once you have used it, put it aside or give it to the facilitator. Points will be scored for each win, and prizes will be awarded to the winning team."

3. The facilitator should write on the chart which team rang first, which rang second, and which rang third.

4. Each group must choose a spokesperson to defend its position.

5. The Judge will call on you in the order of the bells to present your power-card decision. Take turns if possible. One question may be asked for clarification purposes.

6. The Judge makes a decision after hearing all of the reasons. The Judge's decisions are final.

7. Score should be kept on the flipchart.

8. The Judge will declare the winner and explain the correct answer for each scenario. Acknowledge the groups coming in second and third.

9. Pass out prizes.

Step 4: Bring the activity to a close with a brief discussion asking volunteers this question: "What did you learn from this game, and how can it be applied to your job?"

Either end your Power module or move on to the next activity.

POST-ACTIVITY REVIEW

Take time shortly after conducting this activity to reflect on how it went, how engaged the participants were, and what questions they raised. Then, make notes that include how much time you actually spent on the activity.

Scenario Descriptions

SCENARIO # 1

Jill, a manager of operations, says this in a meeting after some minor chitchat:

"Let me start. I have facts and figures here that I received from the comptroller. They show the production costs of our new and improved backyard golf green. I am reasonably sure I can bring in the manufactured cost of this product at $30. I've had a preliminary meeting with my production staff, and they, too, are convinced that these costs are accurate. That ought to make you marketing people happy."

What type of power is Jill demonstrating? How did you arrive at this conclusion?

SCENARIO # 2

At the same meeting, Dolores, the director of finance, says gruffly, "I think that we can cut the costs even lower by doubling the initial run to 100,000 units."

What type of power is Dolores demonstrating? How did you arrive at this conclusion?

SCENARIO # 3

Later in the same meeting, after three different cost-cutting proposals were presented and met with resistance, Jennifer, the director of customer service, says: "We can always cut costs by using cheaper components, but that will only open the door for more service problems. Let's discuss *that* angle while we're on the subject."

What type of power is Jennifer demonstrating? How did you arrive at this conclusion?

SCENARIO # 4

After Jennifer and the others continue to discuss costs, Jill says, "Look, if you put a cheaper motor in the putting green, it will overheat. Our Quality Group has reviewed this product, and it is solid. We can't put a cheaper motor into this product. Changing the motor from the specs I have provided would be a bad decision."

What type of power is Jill demonstrating? How did you arrive at this conclusion?

SCENARIO DESCRIPTIONS (continued)

SCENARIO # 5

Jennifer says, "In light of what you are saying, Jill, I'd like to contact our distributors and assess their repair facilities."

Jill replies, with some controlled anger apparent in her voice, "What do you have against my department servicing the golf green? It's about time we broke precedent and handled the repairs in the right manner. We can do all of the servicing in operations. It fits perfectly with downtime periods, and allows me to use my production workers better. Why should I turn over this 'gravy' work to incompetent distributors?"

What type of power is Jill demonstrating? How did you arrive at this conclusion?

SCENARIO # 6

As the discussion continues, Dolores asks Jill, "What kind of delivery are you anticipating for the new putting green? And when do you plan to make your first shipment?" Jill indicates that her best delivery would be six months from final drawing and prototype delivery to her department. She supports her decision as the conversation continues, by saying: We've never introduced a new product in less than six months. I don't think you people understand all the things that are involved. It may take us a couple of months just to find a supplier for that cheaper motor . . ."

What type of power is Jill demonstrating? How did you arrive at this conclusion?

SCENARIO # 7

Madeline, the marketing director, has been very quiet, which is most unusual for her. She finally says, "I am so pleased that we can move forward with this new product. I have a large number of unused boxes from the earlier model. If we are able to build and design in a way that lets us use the 30,000 boxes we have in the warehouse, I think we'll all be given kudos as a design team."

What type of power is Madeline demonstrating? How did you arrive at this conclusion?

Types of Leadership Power

Type of Power

a. _____   COERCIVE POWER: Based on fear

b. _____   CONNECTION POWER: Based on links with
                     important people

c. _____   EXPERT POWER: Based on the leader's skill and
                     knowledge

d. _____   INFORMATION POWER: Based on access to
                     information

e. _____   LEGITIMATE POWER: Based on position

f. _____   REFERENT POWER: Based on personal traits

g. _____   REWARD POWER: Based on rewards, pay,
                     promotion, or recognition

Power Cards

"Coercive" power   "Connection" power

"Expert" power   "Information" power

"Legitimate" power   "Referent" power

"Reward" power

27

REMEMBER THIS!

A Power Card Affirmation

Overview of Activity

This activity helps the leader expand traditional notions of power by using prewritten "affirmations."

Objectives

→ To creatively explore the use of affirmations.
→ To expand traditional notions of power.
→ To share views on power.

Setting Up the Activity

GROUP SIZE
Any number of participants

ESTIMATED TIME
20 to 30 minutes

TRAINING METHODS
→ Reflection
→ Round-robin activity

MATERIALS
→ Set of "Power Thought Cards" created by Louise L. Hay. (Hay House, 1999 The 64-card boxed deck is available through bookstores and AMAZON - $16.95 a deck.)

➔ Chose two power sayings from the deck of cards and put each on a slip of paper to copy for each person.

EQUIPMENT AND SUPPLIES
➔ Flipchart
➔ Markers

ROOM SET-UP
Tables and chairs in any configuration.

Comments

Affirmations are often helpful as individuals expand their leadership potential, because they remind us of the aspects of our power that need work.

This activity uses a deck of 64 power affirmation cards that consists of several kinds of affirmations (*comfort with one's age, comfort with one's body, belief in balance in life,* etc.). It helps to go through the deck before your session to choose only those cards that you think will help your group concentrate on the subject of power affirmation.

You may write your own set of power affirmations as an option in this exercise. With a new group, it is often easier to begin with prepared cards. Groups that have been working on affirmations and power for some time are often pleased to have the opportunity to create their own affirmation cards.

Trainer's Notes for Activity 27

STEP-BY-STEP PROCEDURE

Step 1: Introduce the activity by asking if anyone has ever used affirmation cards. Have volunteers explain what they think affirmations are. Write responses on the flipchart. (5 minutes)

Step 2: Introduce the concept of affirmations related to power. Say, "Louise Hay created a marvelous deck of 64 cards that she says helps people find their inner strength. I've chosen a few that will help you express yourselves. Let's look at one saying together."

Hand participants the first two-sided card, which reads:

THE POINT OF POWER IS ALWAYS IN THE PRESENT MOMENT

Then ask participants to turn their card over and read the reverse:

The past is over and done and has no power over me. I can begin to be free in this moment. Today's thoughts create my future. I am in charge. I now take my own power back. I am safe and I am free.

Ask, "What does this affirmation say to you? What *action* might you take as a result of this affirmation? Think of a business situation where this affirmation might be useful." Solicit responses.

Step 3: Hold out the stack of cards, and give these directions:

"Randomly take one card and see if it appeals to you. Read both sides and relate it to POWER as you understand the concept from our work today. Take a few minutes to write out the *ACTION* you might take as a result of this affirmation. We will be sharing these out loud with the group. You can ask for a second card if your first card does not resonate with you."

Step 4: After approximately 5 minutes, say, "Let's talk about our reactions to the Affirmations we chose, one at a time." As participants do this, ask, "Who else would like one of these cards?"

Let's all look together at another affirmation.

I CLAIM MY OWN POWER, AND I LOVINGLY CREATE MY OWN REALITY (first side). *I ask for more understanding so that I may knowingly and lovingly shape my world and my experiences.* (second side)

"Again, what does this card mean, as it relates to Power?"

Step 5: Bring the activity to a close with a brief discussion. Ask, "What did you learn from this exercise, and how can you apply it to your job? Will your colleagues think that affirmations are foolish or hokey"? Let volunteers share their responses.

POST-ACTIVITY REVIEW

Take time shortly after conducting this activity to reflect on how it went, how engaged the participants were, and what questions they raised. Then, make notes that include how much time you actually spent on the activity.

28

BALANCE BALLS AND BALANCE LIFE

Overview of Activity

Leaders have a difficult time "juggling" their many work, home, and community projects. This exercise makes this dilemma concrete and encourages reflection and rebalancing of the many priorities of a busy leader.

Objectives

➜ To encourage participants to reflect and talk about what they are doing about "life balance."

➜ To get every participant to participate, so the lesson will be memorable.

➜ To laugh together and enjoy the dilemma of the moment.

Setting Up the Activity

GROUP SIZE
Up to 20 participants

ESTIMATED TIME
30 to 45 minutes

TRAINING METHODS
➜ Role Play
➜ Demonstration
➜ Group discussion
➜ Reflection
➜ Journal writing

MATERIALS
➜ A huge exercise ball, labeled "work"
➜ A basketball, labeled "family"
➜ A medium sized ball (smaller than a basketball), labeled "health and exercise"
➜ A tennis ball, labeled "friends"
➜ A golf ball, labeled "volunteer activities"
➜ A number of bath beads
➜ A length of string or yarn to place on the ball

EQUIPMENT AND SUPPLIES
➜ Assorted colored pens or pencils; markers
➜ Flipchart; stack of blank paper

ROOM SET-UP
Flexible

Comments

New leaders sometimes work so hard to prove their competency that they put their lives out of balance. They leave themselves with little time or energy to do the non-professional activities that are important to them. This exercise is brief, but valuable, because it visually reminds participants of the need for balance in their work and personal lives. It works best with two facilitators but can be adapted for one.

Trainer's Notes for Activity 28

ADVANCE PREPARATION
If there not a second faciliator,

Set up a circle of yarn on the floor, approximately the size of the largest ball. Put all the balls in a basket except the largest one.

STEP-BY-STEP PROCEDURE

Step 1: Ask both facilitators (or substitute with one volunteer) to stand by the circle of yarn. Facilitator 1 holds the largest ball. Facilitator 2 holds the other balls. Facilitator 2 asks Facilitator 1: "With your career totally consuming you, how can you integrate it with the other facets of your life that I know must also bring you joy and fulfillment?"

Facilitator 1 replies, "If the large ball is work, it is impossible."

Step 2: Invite one person to come up and stand in the circle of yarn. Announce that he or she is standing in his or her "circle of life". Pass the biggest ball to this volunteer asking how it feels.

Now give her or him the second ball identifying it as the "family" ball, asking if he or she can manage to hold both at once.

Next adds the third ball identifying it as the "health and exercise ball"

Next add the fourth ball identifying it as the "friends" ball

Next add the fifth ball identifying it as the "volunteer activities" ball

The volunteer starts to get creative about the ways that the balls can be held.

Explain, "When we are totally overwhelmed by all of the facets of our lives, we are sometimes told to take more baths. Now I ask you, is this balance? Is having a little time for *you* the solution?" The facilitator tries to put the bath beads into the volunteer's hands. (They should fall and tumble about.)

Allow time for laughter and random comments. Explain that most new leaders face this dilemma at some time or another—sometimes the first day or week on the job!

Step 3: One facilitator says, "Let's look at what balance really is, because it is different for each of us."

Ask the volunteer to set the balls down in the circle of yarn on the floor. Say, "Please reflect on how your life is balanced now. Take these different parts of your life—all the balls in front of you—and put them into your life."

Step 4: Introduce the concept of the *circle of life* by passing out a piece of paper to each participant and giving the following directions:

"On the blank sheet of paper, draw your life as it is now. For example, draw circles that each represent work, family, recreation, sleep, religious activities, community, and so on. Create circles that are unique to your life." (Make them the size that best represents your reality.)

Step 5: Initiate a discussion with this question: *What is balance, and what is juggling?* Possible answers:

➜ *Juggling* is when there are more balls than time or energy available. Something has to be dropped.

➜ *Balance* is when you feel comfortable with the number of shifting priorities. When you occasionally see that you are out of balance, you know you need to take time to recharge and rebalance your life.

Ask participants to draw new circles of life, but this time size them according to how they would like to balance their lives. When they are done, ask for volunteers to compare and contrast their two sets of circles.

Step 6: To show how this illustration applies to their own situations, explain: "One way to assess how you will find balance is to tie the way you spend your time to your life goals, both personal and professional. I'm giving you two questions to record in your journal." Then say or write the following:

➜ What are your three top goals? Write them on your second chart as a "reflective" bubble.

➜ What changes, if any, do you need to make in your time allotments to achieve your goals?

(Allow some time for this.)

Step 7: Put this quotatoion on the flipchart:

You can have it all; you just may not be able to have it all at the same time. (Oprah Winfrey).

Ask and discuss what this quote means.

Step 8: Conclude the activity by bringing the group outside to toss a few balls around and enjoy a healthy snack. Close on a high note.

POST-ACTIVITY REVIEW

Take time shortly after conducting this activity to reflect on how it went, how engaged the participants were, and what questions they raised. Then, make notes that include how much time you actually spent on the activity.

29

THE TALISMAN
A Symbol for Balance

Overview of Activity

Concrete items that may remind the leader to strive to achieve balance are identified in this module.

Objectives

→ To explore the significance of symbolic objects and their use as reminders.

→ To identify goals that help us achieve balance.

→ To see or reinforce the idea that balance means very different things to different people.

Setting Up the Group

GROUP SIZE
Up to 20 participants

ESTIMATED TIME
20 to 30 minutes, depending on the size of your group

TRAINING METHODS
→ Hands-on activity
→ Round-robin discussion
→ Reflection

MATERIALS

→ Gather common objects that can be imbued with symbolic significance, or provide participants with a list of 2 to 4 objects to bring to the workshop. (The second method generates more involvement.) Objects should not be valuable or have sentimental value, in case something is lost. Here is a sample list to encourage creativity.

→ Aspirin bottle	→ Lightbulb	→ Soap
→ Bottle of water	→ Magazine	→ Spring (from ball point pen)
→ Battery	→ Mirror	→ Tape measure
→ Calorie chart	→ Rubberband	→ Thermometer
→ Candle	→ Salt shaker	→ Toy top
→ Candy bar	→ Seeds	
→ Jump rope	→ Shoelaces	

ROOM SET-UP

Table for objects
Chairs arranged in a circle

Comments

It is very important when developing leadership competencies to do a variety of things to help people remember their accomplishments and achievements. The exercise is quite versatile: It can be used to remind people about competencies after a training session or a discussion. The example we chose to explain is used after a balance activity. How does one remember to maintain balance in one's life? Read on to find out!

Trainer's Notes for Activity 29

STEP-BY-STEP PROCEDURE

Step 1: Introduce the activity by asking , "What is a talisman?" Acknowledge answers. (A sample answer is 'A talisman is a common object that a person chooses to represent something he/she wishes to commit to or accomplish. Then ask, "What do you see as the advantages of a talisman?"

Step 2: "We will now select a talisman for ourselves. We've discussed how to achieve balance in our lives. Pick an object from the table that will remind you of one way that you will strive to achieving balance. (Note: Participants may choose an object other than the one they brought.)

Pick up the object and think about what you will tell us regarding how this talisman can remind you to remember to balance your life's activities."

Step 3: Tell participants that it is time to share ideas.

Ask each participant to briefly explain what they chose and why it "jumped" out at them or captured their attention. For example, "I chose this battery. I am going to put it on my desk, and every time I feel myself running low on energy, I am going to remember that I need a way to recharge myself."

Allow everyone to take a turn, keeping a balance between seriousness and light heartedness.

Step 4: Bring the activity to a close by talking a little about talismans and their importance in a cultural context. Encourage them to use the one they chose today (or one they select later on) to remind them of the importance of balance.

POST-ACTIVITY REVIEW

Take time shortly after conducting this activity to reflect on how it went, how engaged the participants were, and what questions they raised. Then, make notes that include how much time you actually spent on the activity.

30

GROW LIKE A GARDEN

A Metaphor

Overview of Activity

Ways that growing a leader are metaphorically like growing one's garden are explored in this hands-on exercise that includes planting some real seeds.

Objectives

➔ To help leaders compare their development to growing a garden.

➔ To identify key aspects of leadership that participants need to nurture and develop.

Setting Up the Activity

GROUP SIZE
Up to 20 participants

ESTIMATED TIME
30 minutes to 1 hour

TRAINING METHODS
➔ Metaphor
➔ Presentation
➔ Discussion
➔ Hands-on project

EQUIPMENT AND SUPPLIES

→ Bag of dirt
→ Fertilizer
→ Garden gloves
→ Quick-dry spray
→ Seed packets
→ Shovel
→ Spade
→ Pots (one for each person)
→ Variety of small plants
→ Variety of ink stamps and colored-ink pads
→ Watering can

ROOM SET-UP

→ Chairs arranged in a circle facing one table
→ Two to three tables (to hold all of the supplies)

Comments

Consider doing this activity outdoors, especially if you are in a location that would set the mood for gardening.

Trainer's Notes for Activity 30

STEP-BY-STEP PROCEDURE

Step 1: Introduce the topic by explaining that leaders always try to continue developing their skills so they can be the best leader possible, that is, someone who is equipped to lead other people and the entire organization toward their goals.

Tell the group, "I will be giving you a metaphor to help you identify how you can develop yourself as a leader. This will be followed by a crafts project that will help you remember your leadership goals."

Step 2: Provide the group with the gardening items.

Step 3: Present the garden metaphor by saying, "Lay out in front of you the garden items, so that as you talk about each item in your metaphor, you can use it as a prop."

Explain that a metaphor helps us compare two dissimilar objects or ideas in order to understand them better, such as, "Life is like a lemon, because it can be bitter or sweet." Ask for other examples of metaphors.

Step 4: Explain that you have chosen to compare leadership development to gardening. Find out who gardens, so you can draw on their experience during the discussion. Don't tell what is below; try to elicit the answers from them.

Step 5: Develop your metaphor, using the following objects:

→ Garden gloves: These items represent the preparation you must do because you know that gardening and personal development require "down and dirty" work.

→ Bag of dirt: This represents the necessary foundation for growing flowers, trees, and vegetables. Ask participants what an individual's foundation consists of. Answers include one's experiences, education, heredity and learned traits, and financial resources available for development.

→ Seeds: These represent the potential that will grow if properly nurtured.

→ Fertilizer: This represents the boosts that help our development, such as a good coach or mentor, a champion, or sabbatical time to work on professional development.

→ Light and water: Just as we need to know how much light and water our flowers will need, the leader needs to gauge the amount of direction, guidance, and nourishment each employee needs.

→ Shovel and spade: These items represent the tools needed to garden. Ask what tools participants need for their development.

→ Pots: These represent the containers in which things grow. Ask participants what kind of containers contain their growth.

→ Watering can: This item represents the essential ingredient plants need to grow. Ask what their most essential ingredient is that will ensure their success.

→ The sun: This important element represents a manager who provides guidance and nourishment.

Step 6: Spring into action. Have participants move to the tables you have already set up for the craft project.

Continue discussing the garden metaphor as you explain that they are going to spring into action and plant a spring flower: first by "stamping" the pot, and then by adding a plant.

To "stamp" the pots, have participants select stamps that represent their own growth or what they want to develop in themselves: pictures of birds, flowers, the sun, and so on. Demonstrate how to ink the stamp, apply it to the pot, and then clean the stamp afterward. Suggest that they use the quick-dry spray to help speed the process. The pots will need time to dry, so emphasize the importance of patience if you want good results. Don't let them rush through this part of the activity.

Once the pots have dried for a few minutes, have participants move to the second table to add dirt, seeds, plants, and water.

Step 7: Summarize this activity with these words: "Today we had some fun thinking about how our own professional and personal development is like gardening. Put your pot in a place where it will serve as a daily reminder of what you have learned. And don't forget to give it what it needs to grow!"

Discuss how participants can use this same metaphor and the craft project with the people they lead, to help them accomplish their development goals.

POST-ACTIVITY REVIEW

Take time shortly after conducting this activity to reflect on how it went, how engaged the participants were, and what questions they raised. Then, make notes that include how much time you actually spent on the activity.

31

MAKING CONNECTIONS
Networking

Overview of Activity

An effective leader has to network continuously. This module demonstrates how to practice this skill until they become proficient networkers.

Objectives

→ To help leaders understand the importance of continuous networking.
→ To learn and practice networking skills.

Setting Up the Activity

GROUP SIZE
Any number of participants

ESTIMATED TIME
1 hour

TRAINING METHODS
→ Application
→ Discussion
→ Movement
→ Demonstration
→ Writing

MATERIALS
Handout 31.1: *Networking Tools*

EQUIPMENT AND SUPPLIES

→ Index Cards: Three cards per person

→ Self-stick nametags in two colors (two blank nametags for each person, one of each color)

→ Black or dark blue magic markers and pens

ROOM SET-UP
A large room with enough space for people to mill around and practice networking.

Comments

You can present all of the skills included in this activity at the beginning of your workshop, so participants can practice using them during breaks. However, if you conduct a multiday workshop on leadership, consider introducing these skills one at a time—possibly at the beginning of each day, because they are so energizing.

RESOURCES
Baber, Anne, and Waymon, Lynne. *Make Your Contacts Count*. NY: AMACOM, 2002 (also available from www.ContactsCount.com).

Trainer's Notes for Activity 31

STEP-BY-STEP PROCEDURE

Step 1: Start by asking participants to stand and mill around, shaking hands and greeting everyone in the group.

Explain that we are often too hard on ourselves and this can be especially true when we are "networking." When we enter a group for any reason, for example, we don't always feel confident that we will have anything interesting to say to other people, especially if they are strangers.

Step 2: Pass out three index cards to each person. Ask participants to write down three concerns they have about networking, such as "Nobody will talk to me" or "I won't know what to say" or "I can't remember names."

Step 3: Ask everyone to stand up, pick a partner, and hand him or her their three cards. One partner must transform the critical statements to something encouraging, such as "Lots of people will find me interesting, too," or "I always know just what to say," or "I can learn how to remember names." Then reverse and repeat this process.

Explain the importance of changing one's attitude—to start believing that networking will indeed be a positive experience, to stand tall, and to walk confidently into all group experiences.

Step 4: Tell the group that they must start identifying what they want from the connection. Distribute Handout 31.1, *Networking Tools.*

Explain this by saying, "Good networkers are clear about what they need from others, as well as about what they can offer others.

"For example, an individual once told us what her personal agenda was. She said she needed someone who could show her how to transfer data from her computer to her new palm pilot. This same individual identified something she could share with others: 'I just read the best book on networking! Who's interested?' We are going to identify our own agendas, and practice pursuing them with the others in this group."

Step 5: Pass out two different-colored name tags per participant. On one name tag, each participant should write two or three infinitives that answer this sentence stem: "I NEED{{ellipsis}}(to find, to connect with, to create, to learn, and so on)."

Examples: "I'm new in town and need. . . ." or "I'm hoping to find someone who. . . ."

Once participants have completed their first name tags, they should move around and read everyone's tag. When they find someone who can meet their need, they should make note of that person's name and follow up with them later on.

Explain, "Good networkers readily share what they know, who they know, and what they know about that can help others."

"On the second name tag, write down two or three things you have to give other people, such as:

accomplishments
resources
skill
enthusiasm

Then move around and read these new tags. Make notes when you discover someone who has something to offer that you need.

Step 6: Explain that we need to give people a context in which to relate to us, instead of a job title or where we work. For example,

"Hi! I'm Charlotte Waisman. I help women get promotions." When people hear this tag line, they usually ask Charlotte for an explanation. So she elaborates.

Here's another example of what we mean: "Hi! I'm Lois Hart. I help companies save thousands of dollars!" When she is asked, she elaborates as well.

Ask participants to select and work with a new partner to create interesting tag lines for one another.

When everyone is ready, ask people to move around and introduce themselves using their new tag lines.

Step 7: Close the session by asking volunteers to briefly sum up the point of the networking activity.

POST-ACTIVITY REVIEW

Take time shortly after conducting this activity to reflect on how it went, how engaged the participants were, and what questions they raised. Then, make notes that include how much time you actually spent on the activity.

Networking Tools

To be an effective networker, we need to be able to use a few helpful "tools" or skills. This session will focus on learning or practicing how to do four things.

1. Move from Critic to Coach.

When your mental "critic" says something critical or discouraging, transform that negative message into something that will encourage you to move forward.

But my "critic" says . . .
But my coach says . . .

2. Identify your agenda.

Start with the words "*I need or want. . . . ,*" and fill in the blanks. Be specific.

. . . to find	. . . to connect with	. . . to lead
. . . to create	. . . to learn	. . . to understand

Such as, "I'm new in town and need . . ."
Such as, "I'm hoping to find someone who . . ."
Such as, "Do you know someone here who . . . ?"

3. Identify what you can give.

Start by completing this sentence stem: "*I can give . . .*"

. . . accomplishment	. . . resources	. . . leads
. . . skill	. . . enthusiasm	

4. Have a tag line ready.

Create a brief tag line that can be used when you introduce yourself to someone. It will help the other person put you in context, and it will help them remember who you are and what you do professionally.

PART THREE

Set an Example

Leaders must bear one important responsibility when it comes to their own actions. They must instill in others a desire not just to be a leader, but to be *an effective leader*. They must set an example of responsible and effective leadership. Part Three consists of ten activities to help leaders achieve these goals.

Participants in leadership programs have probably completed an assessment such as Myers Briggs or DISC to identify personal styles. They are perhaps familiar with the work of Ken Blanchard, whose *Leader Behavior Analysis II* assesses individual leadership styles. The *Strategic Leadership Type Indicator* (available from HRD Press) is another good tool. Our activity *Flex Your Style* can be used once leaders have determined their dominant styles. It demonstrates how to expand one's style so that behavior can be flexed to better suit more situations.

Leaders also need to help others understand how to handle conflict. The activity *Claim Conflicts* focuses on that particular skill. They also need to empathize with other people, which is the focus of *Walk in Another's Shoes.*

A timeline we call *Where Were You When . . . ?* emphasizes ways to maintain perspective in terms of one's leadership experiences to plan for a better future. *You + Me = A Team* uses symbolism to illustrate how individuals can honor differences, yet still find similarities among colleagues or their teams.

Most people shy away from tooting their own horns. The following activity focuses on the benefits of a little healthy self-promotion.

Public speaking, for some people, is a stronger fear than snakes. *Presenting with Pizzazz!* takes some of the fear out of having to give a formal report or presentation.

In the next activity, *Can We Talk About This? The Leader as Negotiator,* participants are given the opportunity to demonstrate and teach others the skill of negotiation with confidence.

The section concludes with an agenda-setting activity, so that more people can be efficient and effective at facilitating a meeting, followed by an activity that explores ways to use creative and energizing ideas to enhance meetings.

32

FLEX YOUR STYLE

Overview of Activity

Through an art activity, the participants practice the four situational leadership styles identified by Ken Blanchard.

Objectives

→ To practice using the four main leadership styles.

→ To develop an ability to flex one's leadership style and use different styles.

Setting Up the Activity

GROUP SIZE
16 to 24 participants (four groups of 4-6 each)

ESTIMATED TIME
1 hour

TRAINING METHODS
→ Discussion
→ Role play
→ Hands-on art activity

MATERIALS
Handout 32.1: *Let's Make Snowflakes* (one for each group leader)

EQUIPMENT AND SUPPLIES
→ Scissors (two pairs per group)   → Glue
→ Green paper   → "Sparkles"

ROOM SET-UP
A room large enough to accommodate four groups of 4 to 6 people for role play.

Comments

The well-researched Situational Leadership$^{(R)}$ II Model developed by Dr. Ken Blanchard has been used in workshops at all levels to help leaders identify their preferred styles of leading. Before using this activity, we suggest that participants identify their dominant and backup styles by using the Blanchard instrument, *Leader Behavior Analysis II.* The goal is to encourage people to develop flexibility so they can adjust their styles to the needs of those they are leading or to the circumstances.

RESOURCES
Leader Behavior Analysis II Self and *Scoring Profile,* if participants can get feedback from their managers and direct reports (available from Blanchard Training and Development, Inc., 125 State Place, Escondido, California 92029 or 1-800-728-6052).
The *Strategic Leadership Type Indicator* (SLTi) can be used in place of the LBA II. The SLTi is available from HRD Press: 1-800-822-2801, www.hrdpress.com.

Trainer's Notes for Activity 32

STEP-BY-STEP PROCEDURE

Step 1: Introduce the topic by explaining that flexibility, which is a critical leadership competency, is the second skill covered in the Blanchard model. Research data on Blanchard's LBA II profile indicates that 54% of leaders tend to use only one leadership style; 35% use two styles; 10% use three styles; and only 1% are able to use all four styles.

As a leader, you will need to develop the flexibility necessary to effectively meet the needs of those you lead. What did you learn from your *LBA II* score about your ability to be flexible? (The Blanchard Model uses a range of 0 to 30 on flexibility. A score lower than 14 suggests low flexibility because the individual tends to use only one or two of the four main leadership styles. A score higher than 20 indicates high flexibility because the individual uses all four styles more or less equally.)

Step 2: Discuss participants' leadership styles before trying the simulation exercise. Say,

"Think of a time when you led someone and were clearly not flexible in terms of providing the appropriate style for her/his needs. What happened?" (Discuss their responses.)

"Now think about the people you manage. With whom do you tend to use your primary style? Your secondary style?" Discuss.

"Which style(s) do you need to develop?"

Step 3: Introduce the simulation by distributing Handout 32.1, *Let's Make Snowflakes*.

"The purpose of this activity is to give you an opportunity to simulate the behavior of leaders and followers who work in the city's public works department. Your work group has been charged by the Public Works Director with producing artificial snow because the lack of natural snow will spoil the upcoming Winter Fest."

Tell participants, "I have selected a leader for each of four groups: _____ , _____ , _____ , and _____ . Our department quality engineer will be _____ (the facilitator, an extra participant, or a guest).

While I talk with them, I want a volunteer to collect $1 from each of you. Just like real life, this is a competition between teams. The pot will go to the winning team. I also want to talk about the lousy warm fall weather we've been having."

Take the leaders aside and give them their style descriptions, as listed on the handout. Caution them not to reveal the assigned style to their followers.

Step 4: Give additional instructions to the group. Pass out scissors and paper, and restate the goal: "The goal is to see which team can produce the most snowflakes. The winning team will win the pot of money."

Remind them that there are two phases: planning and production. "The planning phase will take 10 minutes, followed by the judging of designs. Then I'll give you 10 more minutes to produce as many snowflakes as you can in that period of time."

Step 5: Begin the planning phase with these instructions: "Your work group has 10 minutes to develop a snowflake design that all members of the team can agree on. You will submit your design for approval to our Quality Assurance Engineer, who is _____ ."

Visit each team and silently listen to what they are discussing. Answer any questions they have, and remind them of how much time is left before judging begins.

Step 6: When time is up, have the leaders deliver their designs for inspection. Give marks according to the criteria, and give $4 as a reward to the team with the best design. Judging is based on:

- Neatness
- Creativity
- Promptness in submitting the design

Step 7: Explain the instructions for this production phase: "Each work group has 10 minutes to produce as many snowflakes as they can before time is called. Each snowflake must be identical to your design. There will be a reward for the work group that produces the most snowflakes. We will start at the same time." (Announce 'Start' when you're ready.)

Visit each team and silently listen to what they are discussing. Answer any questions they have, and remind them of how much time they have left.

When time is up, have them turn in their products for final inspection by the Quality Assurance Engineer. Give marks on the following criteria:

- Neatness of products
- Accuracy in replicating the original design
- Quality control

Present the remaining money as a reward. (Note: You can collect anywhere from $.25 to $1.00 from each participant at the beginning of the session. Just be sure you award 25% of it during the design phase and 75% of it for the production award.)

Step 8: Debrief the simulation, explaining that each leader was asked to behave in a specific leadership style.

Ask followers to share what they experienced and discuss their responses to these questions:

➜ What style (of the four) did you see your leader exhibit?
➜ How did it feel to be led with this style?
➜ Share evidence of that style (what behaviors did you experience?).

> → On a scale of 1–5, how motivated were you?
> → On a scale of 1–5, how productive was your group?

Step 9: Summarize by discussing how the theory can be applied to their leadership responsibilities. Ask these questions:

> → How was this simulation like real life?
> → When is each style most appropriate to use?
> → Which style(s) do you, personally, need to develop?

POST-ACTIVITY REVIEW

Take time shortly after conducting this activity to reflect on how it went, how engaged the participants were, and what questions they raised. Then, make notes that include how much time you ctually spent on the activity.

Let's Make Snowflakes

Role of a Directive Leader

Take charge from the beginning! Let the group members know that you are the boss and that you will tell them what to do. Proceed to outline exactly how the group will design and later produce the snowflakes. Decide on the steps that will be followed, who is to do what, what equipment will be used, and where the activity will be done. If participants have suggestions be polite, but do it your way. Supervise their work very closely.

Role of a Coaching Leader

You will give both direction and support to the group members. Start by explaining your own ideas on how to plan and (later) produce the snowflakes. Listen to everyone's feelings and ideas and keep two-way communication open. However, the final decision will be yours. This is not consensus!

Role of a Supporting Leader

Assume that the members of your group are committed to this task and bring to it useful experience. Therefore, remind them of your confidence in them based on their past performance and tell them that they will jointly decide how to manage this task of planning and producing snowflakes. Emphasize that your role is one of facilitation: You will make sure that they understand the task and know their choices for solving the problem. Although you are their leader, your part and contribution is equal to theirs. Everyone needs to be in agreement or reach consensus on all decisions.

Role of Delegating Leader

Your group has extensive on-the-job experience and is also motivated to get their work done. They have been working as a team for some time now, with the intention of moving toward a self-managed team. Therefore, your role is to explain the task of planning and producing snowflakes. Once they understand their task, delegate the work to them and leave them alone to decide how it will be accomplished. They run their own show and will report in to you when they have questions or are ready to submit their design. Be available; don't leave the room.

33

CLAIM CONFLICT

Overview of Activity

By practicing body language and tone of voice, the participants will recognize how to effectively manage conflict.

Objectives

→ To identify a variety of ways of speaking that can be used to minimize conflict.

→ To use body language to minimize conflict.

→ To provide practice in handling conflict to develop the ability to communicate clearly and directly.

Setting Up the Activity

GROUP SIZE
Any number of participants

ESTIMATED TIME
20 minutes

TRAINING METHODS
→ Demonstration
→ Paired activity

MATERIALS

→ Sets of white, green, and yellow index cards on which is printed an example of either *Message, Tone of Voice,* or *Body Language.* (The *white* cards should each contain a message from the sheet provided. The *green* cards should each contain a different tone of voice from the sheet. The *yellow* cards should each contain a different example of body language from the sheet.) See Job Aid 33.1: *Activity Cards.*

→ Handout 33.1: *Phrases for Practice Rounds*

EQUIPMENT AND SUPPLIES

→ Flipchart
→ Markers

ROOM SET-UP

A circle of chairs

Comments

All leaders, no matter at what level they work in their organization, need to hone their communication skills. Many conflicts can be avoided if leaders carefully select not only the words, but the tone of the message and accompany it with appropriate body language.

Trainer's Notes for Activity 33

STEP-BY-STEP PROCEDURE

Step 1: Introduce the activity by saying, "Communication, especially during conflict resolution, requires an ability to use and interpret carefully both verbal and nonverbal cues. We are going to practice with some examples so that you, as a leader, will be comfortable making your points clearly in a conflict situation."

Distribute Handout 33.1: *Phrases for Practice Rounds.* For Practice #1, divide participants into pairs and have them move their chairs to face one another.

Step 2: Then write this phrase on the flipchart: *Please, try that again!*

"Take turns speaking the following simple phrase, putting inflection or emphasis on a different word in the phrase each time you say it."

Ask them to say this phrase four different ways:

Please, try that again.
Please, *try* that again.
Please, try *that* again.
Please, try that *again.*

Step 3: Debrief by asking participants to respond to these questions:

→ Which worked?

→ Did you have to think of some specific situation to make a true difference in your language style?

Step 4: Begin Practice #2 by saying, "In your pairs, take turns speaking the following phrases, putting inflection or emphasis on a different word in the phrase each time."

a. *You did that well this time.*
b. *Have you read the procedures for this process?*
c. *Is this the result you intended?*
d. *What do you think?*

Step 5: Debrief by posing this question for discussion:

"Why do simple phrases like these get you into trouble during a conflict?"

Step 6: For Practice #3, ask participants to change partners and tell them,

"This time, take turns speaking the same phrases, but put inflection or emphasis on a tone of voice that shows emotion. Listen to the way I can show a different emotion each time for:

Anger (demonstrate)
Interest (demonstrate)
Pleasure (demonstrate)
Apathy (demonstrate)
Distraction (demonstrate)"

Step 7: Debrief by posing these questions for discussion:

Which tones of voice seem to be most valuable? What might be most appropriate?

Which tone is the best one for a leader who is trying to resolve a conflict? Why?

Step 8: "Now, working separately, let us experiment with the three aspects of communication that are affected during conflict resolution: MESSAGE, TONE OF VOICE, and BODY LANGUAGE." Display three stacks of printed cards that are of different colors. Let people choose a card from each pile and demonstrate an example of what the card says. Have participants guess the tone of voice and the body language that is being demonstrated. Then emphasize:

"The message is *what* you are saying, as the earlier examples indicate. The white cards represent the words themselves—the message.

The tone of voice has to do with *how* you are saying what you are saying. This is generally your emotional state. The cards that represent this are green.

Body language refers to what you are showing with your body. As you are talking, are you looking away? Down? Or, in general, looking displeased? Might direct eye contact, nodding your head in approval, or extending your hand to pat the person give a better result? The body language cards here are yellow."

Have participants try another round and decide which interpretations were on-target.

Step 9: Bring the activity to a close by asking,

"Are there instances when your voice, message, or body language has an affect on the conflict? Please share an example with us."

POST-ACTIVITY REVIEW

Take time shortly after conducting this activity to reflect on how it went, how engaged the participants were, and what questions they raised. Then, make notes that include how much time you actually spent on the activity.

Activity Cards

Cut out text message from all three columns and glue each one on a separate card. All the items in the Message column go on white cards; all the Tone of Voice columns go on green cards; and all the Body Language items go on yellow cards.

Message	Tone of Voice	Body Language
"How's it going today?"	Abrupt	Make no eye contact (look down)
"You seem to be doing a great job."	Indifferent	Turn and walk away as you speak.
"Tell me what you think about this situation."	Empathetic	Sit, and lean toward the person. Look into his/her eyes.
"We are glad to have you on our team."	Distracted	Sit, lean back, and put your hands behind your head.
"Does this work meet the standard you have set for yourself?"	Angry	Look around as you say the message.
"What can I do to help you?"	Puzzled	Touch their arm and look them in the eye as you speak.
"Feel free to come to me whenever you have a question or problem."	Genuinely pleased	Cross your arms on your chest as you deliver the message.

Phrases for Practice Rounds

Round #1
Please, try that again!

Round #2

You did that well this time.

Have you read the procedures for this process?

Is this the result you intended?

What do you think?

Round #3

Anger

Interest

Pleasure

Apathy

Distraction

You did that well this time.

Have you read the procedures for this process?

Is this the result you intended?

What do you think?

34

WALK IN ANOTHER'S SHOES
A Diversity Exercise

Overview of Activity

This activity is a hands-on way of practicing diversity in a group setting, so that leaders will gain comfort and experience with the diverse worker population in a real-world work environment.

Objectives

→ To increase empathy for those who are different from ourselves.

→ To provide the opportunity to increase understanding of other people's perspectives.

→ To explore the role leaders play in honoring and respecting diversity.

Setting Up the Activity

GROUP SIZE
Up to twenty-five.

ESTIMATED TIME
1 hour

TRAINING METHODS
→ Reflection
→ Simulation

→ Presentation
→ Discussion
→ Use of analogy

MATERIALS
Pictures, posters, and news clippings that show the different kinds of people who make up our culture

EQUIPMENT AND SUPPLIES
Flipchart and markers

ROOM SET-UP
→ Wall space for a display
→ Tables for small groups

Comments

Invite three to five individuals who represent different demographics of your community or state in terms of race, ethnicity, gender, age, disability, political position, religion to the session.

Pre-workshop assignment: At least two weeks before the session, inform each participant of the pre-workshop assignment described on the next page.

RESOURCE
Advancing Women in Business—The Catalyst Guide Best Practices from the Corporate Leaders, Forward by Sheila Wellington, President of Catalyst (San Francisco: Jossey-Bass) 1998.

Trainer's Notes for Activity 34

PRE-WORKSHOP ASSIGNMENT
Two weeks before the workshop when you will do this activity, send the following instructions to all of the participants.

You will be asked to walk in another person's shoes for two weeks. I have assigned you to "be" the person I've checked on this list:

→ an Asian American
→ a Latino (a)
→ a person with a physical disability
→ a retired person more than 62 years of age

Gather information about life from this person's point of view. Sources might include:

– articles in newspapers or magazines
– stories on the news
– interviews with individuals at work or in your community

STEP-BY-STEP PROCEDURE

Step 1: Introduce the topic by setting the right tone for diversity: Have a bouquet of several kinds of flowers at the front of the room and display a poster or picture of a rainbow. Then pose these questions for discussion:

"How are people like this bouquet of flowers?"

"How do you raise and care for a rose versus an iris?"

"What is the significance of a rainbow to our topic of diversity?"

Then say, "Over the past two weeks, you were to gather information about one type of person. Please do not reveal which person you were researching. Instead, keep that new perspective in the forefront of your mind during this workshop."

Step 2: Switch shoes. Ask participants to place their right shoe on the floor near the refreshments table. Then have each person take one different shoe and wear it during the break (and until further notice).

Step 3: For this next segment on uniqueness, divide the total group into the number of guests you invited (3–5). Tell Group 1 to move to one of the tables you have indicated, where one of the guests is sitting. Do this with each group until everyone is seated. Provide ideas or questions for discussion, such:

➔ *Talk about what you have learned (before the workshop) about your assigned "type" of person.*

➔ *Describe how you are unique—tell something no one else in this group would possibly guess.*

➔ *What is it like to walk in another person's shoes?*

Step 4: Reassemble into the large group and debrief what was discussed at each table. Have someone briefly record some general observations on the flipchart.

Step 5: Facilitate a discussion between your guests and participants by asking these questions of your guests, one by one:

→ Tell about a time when you were excluded from something and what you did about it.

→ What did you feel when you were excluded because of your race or ethnicity?

→ How do you determine if others are treating you differently because of your gender, race, or ethnicity?

→ How often do you think about your race or ethnicity, as opposed to your gender?

→ Were you encouraged to "fit in?"

→ Is it possible for you to "represent" your ethnic or racial group?

Step 6: Now focus on the role of the leader. Ask:

"What is your responsibility for diversity as a leader of a staff or unit?"

"What can you do to influence your organization?"

Step 7: Summary and Closure

Place two flipcharts side by side, and title the first one "Personal" and the second one "Organizational."

Ask participants to describe the consequences and the benefits of improving workplace diversity. Write the responses on the appropriate flipchart, and see if volunteers can help sum up the point of this exercise.

POST-ACTIVITY REVIEW

Take time shortly after conducting this activity to reflect on how it went, how engaged the participants were, and what questions they raised. Then, make notes that include how much time you actually spent on the activity.

35

WHERE WERE YOU WHEN?

A Timeline

Overview of Activity

This module helps each leader chart his or her company's history and significant milestones.

Objectives

→ To encourage participants to take pride in their organizations.

→ To remember the contributions of those who came before us.

→ To identify qualities that will be useful for leadership development.

→ To recognize ways that we are similar to and ways that we differ from one another.

→ To recognize, by seeing history laid out what enormous barriers we have overcome (and what we still have left to do).

Setting Up the Group

GROUP SIZE
Up to 30 participants

ESTIMATED TIME
1 hour (can be expanded if the history identified is a lengthy one)

TRAINING METHODS

➔ Presentation
➔ Discussion
➔ Hands-on activity
➔ Movement
➔ Writing
➔ Reflection

MATERIALS

In advance: A timeline on banner paper showing significant events in the company's history: its founding, points of growth or decline, addition of significant staff people, citations in the media, and so on.

EQUIPMENT AND SUPPLIES

➔ Flipchart
➔ Paper
➔ Markers
➔ Felt-tip pens (fine-point)
➔ Tape
➔ Stars or dots

ROOM SET-UP

The room has to be large enough to accommodate the timeline. People will need to read it and add to it.

Comments

It is important to help your group understand where they have come from and what lies ahead. Looking back on the history of the organization and what people accomplished during its growing stages can be very inspirational.

The timeline can be put up ahead of time if another room is available. This will prevent it from distracting people as you lead other activities.

Trainer's Notes for Activity 35

STEP-BY-STEP PROCEDURE

Step 1: Introduce the activity by saying, "Tell me how your families record their histories." Write brief responses on the flipchart.

Here are some frequent responses that might come up:

→ We have a family Bible in which we record births, confirmations, marriages, and deaths.

→ We have a whole chart that lists our family's genealogy.

→ My mom saved all of my school papers and put them in a scrapbook.

→ I have recorded my grandfather's impressions of growing up.

→ I don't do anything, but I would like to some day.

"For those of you who do not record your history, these are very interesting ways to do it."

"The early histories of some communities in the United States, for example, were written by members of the prevailing religious group. People who were of another religion who played important roles in building the community were deliberately left out of some of these early. The contributions of some people (most notably women and minorities) were not fully recorded. Would our company history go toward making a difference there?"

Group responds.

Step 2: Introduce the idea of having a company timeline. Say, "Help me to put up this timeline that records some of the outstanding achievements in the company."

"Pick up a few dots or stars, and go around and read the chart. Mark ANY achievement that "resonates" with you. We'll take about 20 minutes to do this; don't worry if you don't get to do it all. Start at different points in the timeline, so that you won't all be at the same place at the same time."

Step 3: After about 20 minutes, ask participants to go back to their seats. Say, "I would like one volunteer at a time to go to a highlight on the chart that was particularly moving and share why this is so." Ask one or two more volunteers to do the same.

If it hasn't come out already, be sure to probe for an understanding of how recently things have changed for the company. Ask, "Are any of these achievements related to the history of leaders in the company?"

Step 4: "Now, I'd like each of you to take a red felt-tip pen and mark three events with your name on the timeline that are from *your* own history— events that made you proud of being part of this company. Or, if you are new to the company, mark times when you demonstrated leadership in another company."

"For example you might have been the first person in your family to graduate from college, or your daughter won a national science prize, or you received an unusual promotion. Be sure that at least one achievement is YOURS!"

When participants are done, ask for some of their highlights. (Encourage cheering or applause)

Step 5: "Now take a purple felt-tip pen and put your name on the timeline at a date when you expect to make one important leadership contribution to the company over the next five years." Allow time for volunteers to share.

Step 6: Wrap up the activity by posing this question for discussion:

What was the value of doing this timeline?

POST-ACTIVITY REVIEW

Take time shortly after conducting this activity to reflect on how it went, how engaged the participants were, and what questions they raised. Then, make notes that include how much time you actually spent on the activity.

36

YOU + ME = A TEAM

Overview of Activity

For new teams, this exercise will be especially helpful in team building, as each team draws or creates a team symbol.

Objectives

→ To develop teamwork.
→ To allow participants to reveal their uniqueness.
→ To help instill and encourage leadership.

Setting Up the Activity

GROUP SIZE
Large enough to divide into teams of 5 participants each

ESTIMATED TIME
1 hour

TRAINING METHODS
→ Discussion
→ Reflection
→ Hands-on art project

EQUIPMENT AND SUPPLIES
→ Tables for drawing
→ Chairs

→ Large pieces of paper
→ 8¹/₂″ × 11″ paper
→ Pencils
→ Colored markers or crayons
→ Tape

ROOM SET-UP
Put tables together, if necessary, to provide enough space for team drawing.

Comments

This activity is appropriate for team-building, particularly if you have newly formed IDEA teams. This activity works well because it allows individuals to symbolically reveal a cherished value or belief. There will be some resistance to the art portion, but teams are generally pleased with their results.

One variation is to send people on a walk to find an object that symbolizes who they are or what they believe. Then complete Step 2. Objects that are heavy or impossible to hang may be placed on a spare table.

Trainer's Notes for Activity 36

STEP-BY-STEP PROCEDURE

Step 1: Introduce the activity by asking participants for an example of a time when a team they were on worked extremely well. Ask why they believe it was a high-performance team.

Explain that high-performance teams take time because relationships must first be developed. Indicate that this next activity will demonstrate what you mean.

Step 2: Participants will now create a team symbol. Distribute one 8¹/₂″ × 11″ sheet of paper and a pencil to each person.

Ask participants to think of a symbol that represents who they are as individuals—something they value highly or something that symbolizes an achievement, a special interest, a hobby, or a possession. Allow time for each person to privately sketch his/her symbol on paper.

Step 3: Divide participants into groups of 5. Ask each person to share his/her drawing and explain the meaning of the symbol to the group.

Each small group is to develop one large team symbol or collage. All of the group members' symbols should be incorporated into the new one. They will have to think about what the individuals have in common or develop a theme that applies to everyone.

Ask the groups to label their team symbol with a title or motto and have each member sign the final drawing.

Step 4: Reassemble into the large group and ask each team to explain its symbol. Hang the symbols on the wall nearest to each team's table. Discuss the creative ways people expressed their individuality.

Step 5: Ask participants to identify the advantages of doing an activity such as this one with their own staff or team.

Step 6: Ask for suggestions on other team-building activities (perhaps what people have had experience with), and wrap up.

POST-ACTIVITY REVIEW

Take time shortly after conducting this activity to reflect on how it went, how engaged the participants were, and what questions they raised. Then, make notes that include how much time you actually spent on the activity.

37

TOOT YOUR OWN HORN!

Sell Yourself and Your Ideas

Overview of Activity

Leaders must be sure to share their successes with others. This module helps leaders practice the skills necessary for self-promotion.

Objectives

→ To identify the pros and cons of self-promotion.
→ To create a self-promotion plan.

Setting Up the Activity

GROUP SIZE
20 participants, comfortably

ESTIMATED TIME
1 hour

TRAINING METHODS
→ Discussion
→ Card-sort activity
→ Writing

EQUIPMENT AND SUPPLIES
Flipchart and markers
Sets of cards

MATERIALS
→ Handout 37.1: *Introduction to Self-Promotion*
→ Prepared sets of self-promotion cards (see Job Aid 37.1: *Self-Promotion Cards*)
→ Handout 37.2: *My Personal Board of Directors*

ROOM SET-UP
Tables; chairs arranged so they are facing the flipcharts

Comments

Leaders need to exude confidence and contribute appropriate information. The art of self promotion ensures that just the right amount of information is shared and it is done in a professional manner. This activity helps participants to recognize and use that fine line between saying too little or too much.

RESOURCES
Self-Assertion for Women by Pamela Butler, Ph.D. (NY: Harper Collins, 1992).

Trainer's Notes for Activity 37

STEP-BY-STEP PROCEDURE

Step 1: Introduce the concept of self-promotion by asking participants to list reasons why people should not engage in self-promotion. (Write them on a flipchart.) Tell them to look at the challenge from the standpoint of a prosecuting attorney trying to do away with the practice. Possible arguments include:

- Working hard should be enough.
- My good work will be recognized without me bragging about it.
- It feels like bragging.
- I don't know how to go about it.
- I never thought of it as a necessary part of my career.
- It wastes my time.
- Why would I choose to do this when I have real work to do?
- Others will think I am acting like a politician.
- Others will think I am too aggressive.

Step 2: Divide participants into groups of 4 to 5. Distribute Handout 37.1: *Introduction to Self-Promotion* and ask people to discuss their responses to the questions.

Review the differences among *Passive, Aggressive, and Assertive* behaviors:

- Passive: Say nothing, hint around the subject, and do nothing directly.

- Aggressive: Attack the person, moralize, and use put-downs.

- Assertive: Directly and honestly express your own feelings and opinions.

Step 3: Now explore the advantages of self-promotion by making a defense lawyer's case as to why self-promotion is a good thing. Write the ideas on a flipchart. Possible answers include:

- We need to be able to ask for what we want.

- There is value in having allies in the workplace.

- Appropriate self-promotion is a proactive strategy that enhances our careers.

- We need to display our skill because others may not be observant.

- The more I know about the business and its leaders the more effective my contribution will be.

- Self-promotion is an important skill and might be a necessary part of my overall plan as a leader.

- Other successful leaders are political.

- I can be appropriately political and assertive.

Step 4: Remind participants that they have heard prosecution and defense arguments. Now ask them for their "verdict." "How do we find on the issue of self-promotion—for the Prosecution or for the Defense?" (Note: In all the times we've done this activity, the Defense has won!)

Step 5: Summarize the verdict, and return to the arguments in favor of using it as a leadership strategy. "Because we agree that self-promotion has some value, we will now take time to develop a plan to promote ourselves."

Steps to develop a Self-Promotion plan

1. Review which aspects of self-promotion will contribute to leadership development. Pass out sets of cards each one bearing a different title from the list below. Ask participants to put the cards in three piles: the

things they do well already; the things that are critical to develop immediately; and those to consider in the future.

2. Set goals that are specific and measurable.

   Provide an example: *My goal is to "get noticed" twice as often for my exceptional work. This could include a verbal mention to the Board or management, a write-up in the company newsletter, or a congratulatory note sent by the boss.*

   Ask participants to write goals for those categories in the "Critical" pile.

3. Develop a "Personal Board of Directors" for yourself.

   Facilitator: Distribute Handout 37.2: *My Personal Board of Directors,* telling participants:

   "Think about all the people you know from work: colleagues, managers, administrative assistants, customers, vendors, industry experts, trade association members, and leaders who influence others. Identify key people who have a broad base of knowledge that can complement your own. Use the handout to make your lists.

   "Develop a plan for enhancing a relationship with these people. Get on a committee they chair, join a community organization they are interested in, ask them to speak to your team or professional trade organization, or call and ask for a meeting to learn more about their area of the business."

   Develop a set of questions around industry trends, technology innovation, or regulatory impact, and ask for their opinions. When you ask good questions and they do all the talking, you become known as a great conversationalist.

   "Write down what you plan to do with the people on your lists." (Allow 25 minutes for this step.)

Step 6: Bring the activity to a summary close, asking the group: "What other ideas do you have for increasing your visibility?"

   Remind people that the goal is to form a permanent Board of Directors for your personal use that includes people who want a collaborative exchange.

Relate the idea of self-promotion to leadership. Ask participants to review how self-promotion can be a useful leadership tool.

POST-ACTIVITY REVIEW

Take time shortly after conducting this activity to reflect on how it went, how engaged the participants were, and what questions they raised. Then, make notes that include how much time you actually spent on the activity.

Introduction to Self-Promotion

The "case" against self-promotion must be made. Answer the following questions:

1. Why do I think I should *not* engage in self-promotion?

2. What is it about self-promotion that makes me uncomfortable?

3. How might I look at self-promotion from a new perspective?

4. What new information would help me reconsider my assumptions regarding the practice of blowing my own horn?

5. Does completing this review change my thinking about whether or not I should promote myself?

Self-Promotion Cards

Knowledge

Information

Get noticed

Support

Influence

Get promoted

Awareness

Internal reputation

Skills are utilized

My Personal Board of Directors

Identify people in key positions or with key expertise whom you currently know.

Name   My plan for contact with them

_____

_____

_____

_____

_____

_____

_____

_____

_____

Identify people in key positions or with key expertise whom you do not know.

Name   My plan for more contact with them

_____

_____

_____

_____

_____

_____

_____

_____

_____

38

PRESENTING WITH PIZZAZZ!

Overview of Activity

Leaders always present their ideas to others. In this activity, many ideas are offered to enhance the public speaking opportunity.

Objectives

→ To review proven techniques that will enhance presentations.

→ To provide an opportunity to use these techniques to deliver short presentations.

Setting Up the Activity

GROUP SIZE
Up to fifteen participants

ESTIMATED TIME
→ 1 hour for tips
→ 10 minutes per person to practice deliveries

TRAINING METHODS
→ Presentation
→ Assessment
→ Demonstration
→ Discussion

MATERIALS

→ Three colored signs labeled *Excellent, Good,* and *Fair*

→ Five colored signs labeled *Confidence, Organization, Introductions and Conclusions, Visual Aids, and Delivery*

→ Copies of Handout 38.1: *Take-Home Assignment*

→ Handout 38.2: *Feedback Sheet for Public Speaking.*

EQUIPMENT AND SUPPLIES

Flipchart and markers
Five tables

ROOM SET-UP

Chairs arranged in a circle, facing flipcharts

Comments

A leader will give many speeches over the course of his or her career, but leaders have only one opportunity to make a stunning impression. This is why it is so important to regularly review proven techniques that make presentations meaningful and memorable. This activity is best done in two sessions: one to explain the concepts and a second to perform the speeches and get feedback.

Trainer's Notes for Activity 38

STEP-BY-STEP PROCEDURE

Step 1: Introduce the activity by explaining how important it is to be able to deliver effective presentations.

"As a leader, you will give innumerable speeches over the course of your career—in your organization, as well as in the community. Presenters have only one opportunity to make a stunning impression, so we are taking some time today to review techniques that make presentations meaningful and memorable. You will learn how to add pizzazz to *all* of your presentations!

First we will share our experiences listening to presentations that missed the mark and try to determine what we want to avoid. Then we will examine what you already know about making a good presentation, and we will review any "tried-and-true" tips that will add life to your talks.

Then, I will give you an assignment to prepare a presentation that you will deliver to this group the next time we meet."

Step 2: "We all have suffered through ineffective and boring presentations. Can anyone remember an especially memorable one that went over like a lead balloon?" Allow a few minutes for people to share experiences, and then ask

"What is it about some speakers that can turn an audience off? Let's make a list of things that speakers do wrong."

Note a few observations on the flipchart, and then ask how many things on this list have to do with content. The participants should see that most mistakes have nothing to do with content, yet most of the planning time is spent on content. "Today we will focus on your delivery."

Step 3: Write the following facts on a flipchart page.

Where does the real impact of a message come from?

7% comes from your words.
38% comes from your tone of voice.
55% comes from nonverbal communication.

Discuss how people feel about these research findings, and explain that when we communicate by phone, the percentages shift: tone of voice is said to make up 80 % of what is conveyed!

Step 4: Explain that you will now give people a chance to look at their own performances.

Lay out the three colored signs (*Fair, Good, Excellent*) on the floor, each 6 to 10 feet apart.

Ask everyone to stand up and listen to a question posed by you. They should then move to the colored sign that most closely fits how they rate their presentation skills. Follow this same procedure for all five questions, and encourage them to keep a record.

The questions are:

How do you rate your level of comfort and confidence in delivering presentations?

How do you rate your ability to organize the content of a presentation?

How do you rate your ability to create an enticing introduction and a compelling conclusion?

How do you rate your use of visual aids to enhance your presentations?

How do you rate your energy during the delivery of your presentations?

Step 5: Now give people time to share what they know about presentations. Start by putting one of the colored signs at each of five tables (*Confidence, Organization, Introductions and Conclusions, Visual Aids, and Delivery*).

Tell each participant to decide to which of these five areas they will be contributing suggestions. Encourage people to select one of their highest rated areas, but it is fine if they have ideas relating to areas in which they are weak. Let them chose the area.

Participants should divide into small groups according to the area they have chosen to focus on and use the flipchart paper and markers to list the ideas the group will suggest.

When everyone is finished, each group will present its suggestions. Embellish what they present with your own tips. Here are a few:

Step 6: Tips on Making Good Presentations

Enhance your confidence.

Gather all the information you can about your audience's knowledge of the content, the setting, and the equipment you plan to use.

Step 7: Now do some visualization. Ask participants to close their eyes and think of a very good speaker they know. Ask, "What is the expression on his or her face? What gestures are used? Does he or she move around while talking? Is there any use of visual aids? Move forward until the speech is done. What are the audience's reactions?

Keep your eyes closed. Now remove the face of this speaker and put yours on the body. Make your facial expressions animated. "Watch yourself making gestures. See yourself moving around a little, but not pacing. Look out at the audience and see how well they are responding. Give a strong conclusion, and listen to the applause."

Suggest that they visualize several times as they plan and practice their presentations. Tell them that closing their eyes prevents distraction.

Step 8: "When it comes time to deliver your presentation, get to the meeting room early. Check the equipment. Walk around. Greet people as they arrive and chat with them."

Here are more tips:

→ Start planning and organizing as early as possible.

→ Review your outcomes and what you know about the audience and the room site.

→ Create your outline to include:

  ■ Purpose
  ■ Organization
  ■ Introduction
  ■ Conclusions
  ■ Delivery choices
  ■ Visual aids

→ Memorize your opening and conclusion.

→ As for your delivery, practice, practice, practice!

→ Exercise just beforehand: Sit in a chair and press your hands together. Sit in a chair and push your feet to the floor. In the chair, put your hands on the seat, and push down-pull up.

→ Use positive affirmations, such as *"Today my message will impact others!"* The purpose is to reverse the negative talk that our inner critic supplies.

→ Stand, and you will get better results. Do not stand behind a lectern or podium, however; stand to the side. Use cards to remind you of important points.

→ Move to a different location, such as back and forth between two charts or two flipcharts. Avoid the "pacing lion" syndrome, because it is very distracting.

→ Draw people in by making eye contact. Vary your eye contact so you connect with everyone.

→ Use gestures above the waist—no hands in pockets or behind your back. Watch actors on TV with the sound off, and see how they move.

➔ Get and keep mental attention. Every nine minutes, our attention wanes. Here are some ways to hold their attention:

- Use people's names when they ask a question.

- Give quizzes.

- Stop and ask them to compare notes with a neighbor.

- Refer to a well-known event, movie, quote, or person (or all).

- Use a "stand-up" poll.

- Tell audiences that you will be giving them a gift a little later. (But be sure you do it.)

Step 9: Tips on Using Visual Aids

➔ Keep them simple—six lines per screen, maximum.

➔ Use color.

➔ Stick to one subject per visual.

➔ Don't reveal the aid until you are ready to use it.

➔ Use blank flipchart pages between pages you write on.

➔ Write notes to yourself in pencil on the flipchart page.

➔ Turn off equipment when not in use.

➔ Look at the audience—not the aid. Don't read out loud what people can read themselves.

➔ Don't pass things around during the presentation.

Step 10: You told participants that you would be giving them an assignment so each person can apply these tips when they deliver a presentation at a later time. Distribute Handout 38.1: *Take-Home Assignment.*

Step 11: Follow-up session for participant presentations.

Set the stage by arranging chairs to simulate a meeting room.

Draw straws to determine who goes when.

Distribute a feedback sheet to each participant. Tell participants that they will evaluate the person who speaks just before they do. As facilitator, you should evaluate each person.

For each round:

→ The presenter gives a six-minute speech.
→ Provide time for listeners to complete feedback sheets.
→ Lead a feedback session.

Distribute Handout 38.2: *Feedback Sheet for Public Speaking.*

POST-ACTIVITY REVIEW

Take time shortly after conducting this activity to reflect on how it went, how engaged the participants were, and what questions they raised. Then, make notes that include how much time you actually spent on the activity.

Take-Home Assignment

Be prepared to speak to us for six minutes on the topic _____ .
For example, "How I make sure that balance and play fit into my life." Plan
to use at least one visual aid. The purpose of this presentation is to share
strategies that might be helpful to each of us, as well as to give us a glimpse
of your presentation style and your ability to put into use the elements we
have outlined in "Presenting with Pizzazz."

Feedback Sheet for Public Speaking

Your name: _____ Speaker's name _____

Date: _____

Award points for each item in the category, using a 1–5 scale (5 is excellent)

Development of Introduction

    Gains attention _____

    Establishes rapport _____

    Discloses purpose _____

    Motivates _____

Organization of Speech

    Clear _____

    Simple _____

    Easy to follow _____

Focus: Body of Speech

    Uses a variety of supporting materials _____

    Uses audiovisual aids appropriately and effectively _____

    Uses reinforcement techniques _____

Speaker's Body Language

    Facial expressions _____

    Use of eye contact _____

    Use of gestures _____

    Posture and movement _____

Speaker's Voice

    Clear _____

    Varied _____

    Rate of speech varied appropriately _____

Conclusion of speech/Overall effectiveness _____

39

CAN WE TALK ABOUT THIS?
The Leader as Negotiator

Overview of Activity

Negotiation is the skill that leaders will use more than any other. By taking roles in a work scenario, leaders practice this critical competency.

Objectives

→ To identify participants' preferred negotiation styles.
→ To practice using negotiation skills.

Setting Up the Activity

GROUP SIZE
Negotiation teams of 5 participants each

ESTIMATED TIME
1 to 2 hours

TRAINING METHODS
→ Application
→ Self-assessment
→ Case study
→ Coaching
→ Presentation
→ Discussion

MATERIALS
➜ Handouts 39.1, 39.2 and 39.3: *Background for Roles of Maura, Judith, and Greg*
➜ Handout 39.4: *Preparation for Negotiation*

EQUIPMENT AND SUPPLIES
➜ Flipchart
➜ Markers
➜ Extra paper and pens

ROOM SET-UP
Tables and chairs for small groups

Comments

Leaders use negotiation more than any other leadership competency. Training people in negotiation skills, however, is challenging, because you have to change people's behavior—not just give them information. And that takes time. A module or two about negotiation won't be particularly useful in the long run unless participants understand the concepts and practice them frequently. Some people are natural negotiators, but everyone can improve with practice and reflection.

In this book, we have outlined ways to create and deliver the leadership training modules. In this activity, we use a coach for each negotiation team. This approach allows dispassionate observers to help identify roadblocks or issues that must be addressed. The best negotiations are those in which each "side" feels that it has "won." Negotiation is *not* compromise!

This module requires that you do some advance preparation. Have participants take the *Dealing with Conflict Instrument* (DCI) so they understand their chief negotiation style; they will then feel comfortable changing their negotiation strategies. We chose this instrument after reviewing an array of assessments because the five style types identified in the DCI parallel the negotiation styles commonly accepted by leaders. It is important that facilitators know how to use the DCI instrument, which won't be difficult to do since the instrument itself comes with detailed instructions for training and teaching. This instrument is also useful for other kinds of training.

We recommend that your participants complete the instrument before the module is presented, and then bring the scored instrument to the session.

RESOURCE
The *Dealing with Conflict Instrument* by Alexander Watson Hiam, 1999 (Amherst MA: HRD Press 1-800-822-2801 or www.hrdpress.com)

Trainer's Notes for Activity 39

STEP-BY-STEP PROCEDURE

Step 1: Introduce the subject of negotiation by asking, "What is your definition of negotiation in your business context?" Elicit answers and write them on the flipchart.

Now ask participants if they know what their personal negotiation style is based on. Discuss responses.

Then tell participants, "Negotiation is one of the most complex leadership competencies. You have all taken the *Dealing with Conflict Instrument.* Let's chart your primary conflict styles." Ask for scores, and write them on the flipchart.

Step 2: Then say, "Now, what do these scores mean? I believe that bargaining and negotiation styles are relatively stable. They are personality-driven clusters of behaviors and reactions that arise in negotiating encounters. Bargaining and negotiation strengths are those in or above the 75th percentile.

Step 3: Use the flipchart to review the main points.

Accommodators. Negotiators who are strongly predisposed toward accommodating derive significant satisfaction from solving other people's problems. This is a great trait to have on a negotiating team. If you are weak in terms of accommodation, you might not be interested in the other party's emotional state, needs, or circumstances. You might also try to hold out for more of what you want.

Compromisers. Negotiators who are eager to close the gap in a fair and equitable way. However, strong compromisers often rush the negotiations. Weak compromisers are often men and women of great principle. They can sometimes appear to be stubborn.

Avoiders. Negotiators who are adept at deferring and then dodging the confrontational aspects. Diplomats and politicians are often high avoiders. Low avoiders are sometimes perceived as lacking tact, and as negotiators tend to show a high tolerance for assertive, hard-nosed bargaining.

Collaborators. Negotiators who tend to enjoy negotiations because they enjoy solving tough problems. They are instinctively good at using negotiation to probe beneath the surface of a conflict.

Competitors. Negotiators who, like high collaborators, like to negotiate, but they enjoy it for a different reason: Negotiation presents an opportunity for them to win what they consider to be a game based on a set of practiced skills. People who are weak in the competing area tend to think that negotiations are all about winning and losing.

Now that you have outlined the five basic styles, tell participants that there is no single correct style for being a strong negotiator.

Step 4: Divide the group into five-person teams. Each team will do its own role play, but the entire group will reassemble to discuss differences in the way participants negotiated.

Explain the instructions, as follows:

"We are now going to divide into teams and practice negotiating. Each team of five will consist of three players, one coach, and one recorder. While the players will be the primary spokesmen and do the actual negotiating, the recorder on the team will take notes regarding content, so you have a record of the experience. The recorder will have access to all three player background sheets and will talk about content during the debrief. The coach has a critical role: He or she is the primary helper in the negotiation process, and can call brief time-outs to advise the negotiators.

"At the end, we'll take some time to debrief and discuss all of these roles."

Let team members decide who will take on which role. Once they have selected their roles, distribute either Handouts 39.1 39.2, or 39.3, *Background for Roles of Maura, Judith, and Greg.* Each player gets to see only the scenario he/she is going to play, but the recorder and coach should have a copy of each.

Step 5: After they have read their role's description, distribute and have each player complete Handout 39.4: *Preparation for Negotiation,* while you meet with the recorders and coaches to explain their responsibilities. Let the teams go off by themselves to play out the scenario (about 20 minutes).

Step 6: When the role-playing is completed, debrief together.
Recorders start the debrief, explaining what they recorded of the negotiation. (Chart the highlights of each group's process.) Since you only have two hours, divide the time up evenly so each group has

approximately the same amount of time to respond. Recorders will be asked to describe:

→ *"BATNA"* (*Best Alternative to a Negotiated Agreement*): This is a way for the recorder to try to identify what Maura, Judith, and Greg were really ready to settle for (before the negotiation), vs. what they got as a result of the negotiation.

→ *"WW"* (*What did I win?*) In the recorder's opinion, what did each person gain?

→ *"DD"* (*What would I do differently?*) The recorder reviews each role and identifies moments when Maura, Judith, and Greg might have made different decisions.

Step 7: When the recorders have finished, the coach makes a report, concentrating on his or her role during the negotiation. The coaches should answer these questions:

→ When did you stop the scenario? Why?
→ How were you helpful?
→ Did you add to a feeling that the negotiation was successful?

Then the coaches should identify each of the three conflict styles used by the team. If the individual's primary style is to accommodate, they will still use that style to flesh out a role—even though they are role-playing.
  If there is still time, allow the role-players in the group to comment on the experience.

Step 8: Summarize the activity by asking participants, "As a result of this foray into negotiation, what are you going to do about your negotiation style?" Encourage discussion in teams or in the whole group. Have participants take notes on how they can apply what they learned about negotiation styles.

POST-ACTIVITY REVIEW

Take time shortly after conducting this activity to reflect on how it went, how engaged the participants were, and what questions they raised. Then, make notes that include how much time you actually spent on the activity.

Background Information

Maura (*Director of Research*)

Your colleague Greg has worked in your department for three years. Although it has always been company policy that a staff member may progress and move from one department to another, this has only been done when you encouraged the move. Part of this comes from the fact that you have been with the company the longest and can most clearly see how the departments interact.

This time, Judith (the director of operations) asked Greg if he would be willing to move to her department—without discussing it with you. Judith then calls you, but the conversation doesn't go well, and you believe a face-to-face meeting is critical. She needs another person and thinks that this would be a good career move for Greg.

This upsets you, because Greg is a very valuable part of your department. He understands the current issues, as well as the difficulties involved in getting out the current product. There is no one else on your staff who shares this strength. You know that you can leave the details to Greg, and he will take care of any outstanding issues. Greg has also been your point person when it comes to training each new member of the department.

Greg just called to tell you that Judith has asked both of you to go to a meeting to finalize the particulars of Greg's move. The meeting will take place later today. It isn't entirely clear from the conversation, but you think Greg is upset. As you briefly discuss the meeting with Greg, you tell him that you don't want him to leave the department.

You now realize that expressing your own disappointment at the prospect of losing him might look like you are not supportive of his career advancement.

As part of your preparation for the meeting, you go to Helen, the director of human resources, for her suggestions. (This is not "actually" done but gives you the chance to embellish details. What you discover there is known only to you.)

Take a few minutes to prepare for the meeting in Judith's office. (Use the preparation worksheet.)

Background Information

Judith (*Director of Operations*)

You have a vacancy in your department. It is company policy to first look within, to encourage lateral and promotional moves. You have noticed that Maura has increasingly been relying on one of her staff members, Greg, to maintain the efficient inner workings of her department. It is clear to you that Greg is very competent and enjoys the additional responsibilities given to him.

You believe that Greg deserves a chance for promotion. In order to be considered, you think he should work in several other departments, and probably get some additional formal training as well. It seems logical to you to suggest that Greg make the move. It's part of the company policy, and Greg certainly meets the criteria for advancement.

You call Maura to discuss it and tell her that you have been giving it serious consideration. You were met with silence. This didn't surprise you: You long suspected that Maura deliberately blocked a few other transfers. You don't know if anyone has tried to get Greg to transfer to another department before now, but you think Mary (director of quality) was interested at one time.

You are on your way down the hall to ask Mary for some background and to talk with Maura about this issue, when you run into Greg. You make a "spur-of-the moment" decision to tell him that you are going to move him, preempting Maura's "permission." You also tell Greg to call and inform Maura and then the two of them should come to your office to discuss the details.

You then go off to Mary's office to try to understand the background. (This is not "actually" done but gives you the chance to embellish details. What you discover there is known only to you.)

You feel guilty that you didn't talk it through properly with Maura, but you know that she would not have been receptive. You believe that the transfer is clearly best for Greg.

Take a few moments to prepare for the meeting with Maura and Greg in your office. (Use the preparation worksheet.)

Background Information

Greg (*currently a scientist*)

You have worked in the same department since coming to the company about three years ago. You thoroughly enjoy your work. Some people have been moved to other departments, but Maura has consistently given you more and more responsibility, sees that you are well-compensated and makes sure that you get bonuses and training opportunities.

The additional responsibilities have kept you from becoming bored with your position, and in a true sense, you have learned some of the detailed inner workings of the department. In fact, you probably have more "hands-on" knowledge than Maura does. She counts on this when she asks you to handle the orientation of new staff members. She has also had you act as liaison to the director of quality (and you have established a very close working relationship with Mary, the director).

When Judith sees you in the hall and tells you that she intends to transfer you, you are flabbergasted. You have found your niche working with Maura, and you believe that it is in your best interest to stay.

If you don't stay there, the next-logical move is to go to Mary's department because she knows your work and your capabilities, and you believe that she would treat you well.

You don't feel that you can refuse the offer to move to Judith's department, because it is part of company policy that you should be willing to move. You are very upset to think that Maura didn't say anything to you about the move and didn't protect you from having to make the move. Judith asked you to contact Maura, and when you call her you learn that she wasn't conniving behind your back, and she actually wants you to stay.

You are confused. You go to Mike, a member of Judith's department, to try to understand Judith. (This is not "actually" done but gives you a chance to embellish details. What Mike tells you is known only to you.)

Use the preparation worksheet to get ready for the meeting that will take place in Judith's office.

Preparation for Negotiation

1. Identify your opening position clearly for yourself, as you understand it:

2. If I say yes to the transfer, what have I gained? What have I lost?

3. If I say no to the transfer, what have I gained? What have I lost?

4. Identify at least three advantages and three disadvantages for each position you take.

5. What are at least two additional options you can invent and discuss in the meeting (without really committing to them)?

6. What is at least one thing you can do to separate the "people" from the problem?

7. What information did I gain in my private conversation, and how can it be useful in the negotiation?

8. Answer the following for yourself, "This is the best decision because. . . ."

40

THE AGENDA

A Leader's Guide to a Great Meeting

Overview of Activity

While this might be seen as a very basic skill, some leaders have never learned the practical tips for creating agendas that make a meeting successful.

Objectives

→ To demonstrate how to create a useful agenda.
→ To identify the value of creating and using agendas.
→ To practice creating an agenda.

Setting Up the Activity

GROUP SIZE

Any number of participants that can be divided into groups of 5

ESTIMATED TIME

1 to 1½ hours

TRAINING METHODS

→ Presentation
→ Demonstration
→ Case study

MATERIALS
Handout 40.1: *Sample Agenda*

EQUIPMENT AND SUPPLIES
→ Flipcharts (one per small group)
→ Markers
→ Self-sticking notes

ROOM SET-UP
Space for a table, chairs, and flipchart for each small group

Comments

It is important to develop and distribute an agenda before a scheduled meeting, because it gives people time to gather information about important issues. It also ensures that the most-important topics will be discussed at the meeting.

RESOURCES
For more on other facilitation techniques, read *Faultless Facilitation—A Resource Guide*, by Lois B. Hart (Amherst, MA: HRD Press) 2001.

Trainer's Notes for Activity 40

STEP-BY-STEP PROCEDURE

Step 1: Introduce the topic with these remarks:

"If we look back at meetings we've attended or conducted that have not been too successful, we are likely to conclude that not having an agenda or having only a poorly planned one was a major reason why the meeting was a flop. The focus of this next activity is on how to prepare a good agenda.

In this activity, we will also review why it's important to have an agenda. You will have an opportunity to work in small groups to prepare one agenda together."

Step 2: Discuss the importance of having an agenda for every scheduled meeting. List participants' ideas on the flipchart. Make sure they realize that agendas:

→ Clarify which tasks and issues need discussion.
→ Put items into an order for discussion.

→ Help to identify how much time will be needed for a meeting.

→ Provide a way to measure the accomplishment of tasks.

→ Provide an outline for writing a report after the meeting.

State how to prepare an agenda. Discuss and record on the flipchart the pros and cons of preparing the agenda before the meeting:

1. Pros:

> → It saves time in the meeting.
>
> → Items can be put in logical order.
>
> → Group members can prepare and bring resource materials to support items on the agenda.

2. Cons:

> → It reduces spontaneity.
>
> → Participants cannot decide whether or not all of the items are important for a particular meeting.

Step 3: Tell participants that the next 45 minutes will be spent putting together a sample agenda. Then present the challenge: To set up an agenda for a two-hour problem-solving session. Here's the scenario:

"You work in a manufacturing setting. It has come to your attention from several sources that the sales department makes promises to customers that cannot be kept under the current production schedule. You are calling a meeting with key people from sales, production, shipping, information technology, and sales support departments. Your goal is to solve the problem of scheduling so your company can keep its promises to customers."

Distribute Handout 40.1, *Sample Agenda,* and go over the parts of an agenda:

→ Date and time of meeting

→ Names of those serving as team leader, facilitator, and recorder

→ Goals and objectives for the meeting

→ Topics, issues, and or activities

→ Processes to be used

→ Name of person responsible for each part of the agenda

→ Time allotted for each item on the agenda

Step 4: Divide participants into teams of three, and give each trio one large sheet of chart paper and a pad of 3" x 3" self-sticking notes. At the top, they must write the goal of the meeting, as well as starting and ending times.

Demonstrate how to use the chart paper to sketch out the agenda's skeleton. Use one sticky note for each component of the agenda. Start with the normal items included in an agenda, such as

➜ Introductions
➜ Administrative details
➜ Breaks
➜ Closure

Each team should use the self-sticking notes for these items, and place them on the paper. Show them on the flipchart how this is done:

Each team should first brainstorm all of the parts of this two-hour meeting. For each topic or issue, they should prepare a separate sticky note, which is physically placed on the large agenda sheet they are designing. Encourage people to move items around until they get a flow that makes sense and that provides some variety to the agenda, while still accomplishing their goal. Tell them that agenda items are commonly listed down the left of the page, in one column.

Step 5: When all the teams finish, post the agendas where everyone can see and discuss each design. You are likely to see different designs that can achieve the same goal. Praise creativity and variety of methods used in the design.

Step 6: Review agenda basics, and be sure you include these tips:

➜ Stick to your agenda as much as you can. Periodically review what you think has been accomplished, and preview which items are left. Make adjustments as needed, using group consensus. Make sure you keep to the announced times for breaks and adjournment.

➜ It is very common to end up with too many items on an agenda, so don't be surprised when everything isn't covered. Summarize those items that weren't covered, and decide with the group whether they can be accomplished by an individual or a sub-group, or held until the next meeting. Make a record of this decision, so individuals or sub-groups can give reports at the next meeting. Also note the items that will be incorporated into the next agenda.

➜ The agenda can be used as an outline for preparing the minutes of the meeting or a similar report.

Example #1

Name of Organization or Group
Date
Time
Place

AGENDA
Goal or Objective: To Keep Our Promises

Introduction

Warmup to problem-
solving (2 minutes)

Break (7 minutes)

Agenda item

Agenda item

Summary

Closure

Step 7: Summarize the importance of having a well-planned agenda with the following words:

"Remember: An agenda is the roadmap you need to reach your chosen destination."

POST-ACTIVITY REVIEW

Take time shortly after conducting this activity to reflect on how it went, how engaged the participants were, and what questions they raised. Then, make notes that include how much time you actually spent on the activity.

Sample Agenda

Name of team:
Date and time of meeting:
Place of meeting:

Department or team:
Facilitator:
Recorder:

Goal:
Objective:

I.	Introductions:	Mark Naismith, Director of Operations	(5 minutes)
II.	Review of November meeting:	Jan Smity, Chair of Task Force Committee	(5 minutes)
III.	The Year Ahead: The Company's New Product Line	Vera Jamison, Vice President of New Product Development	(20 Minutes)
IV.	Selection of Markets We Will Focus on in 2003	Mark Naismith	(Discussion and vote: 25 minutes)
V.	Summary and Close		

41

ENERGIZE!

Review of Activity

When a team or staff work together for long periods of time, they should be encouraged to take frequent energy breaks to keep their ideas flowing. This exercise helps to increase their energy. It also includes other practical tips on the use of snacks, water, and physical activity to achieve this goal.

Objectives

→ To present ways to reenergize and keep the ideas flowing.
→ To try some of these ideas in an informal setting.

Setting Up the Activity

GROUP SIZE
Any number of participants who will be sorted into 4-5 per group

ESTIMATED TIME
1 hour

TRAINING METHODS
→ Discussion
→ Demonstration
→ Movement

MATERIALS

Fresh fruit for snacks

EQUIPMENT AND SUPPLIES

→ One flipchart per group of four to five (or sheets of paper on the wall for small groups)

→ Sticky notes

→ Variety of CDs and a CD player

ROOM SET-UP

Leave space along the walls so the small groups can stand next to the flipcharts.

Comments

Our energy tends to ebb and flow. The tasks at hand might be critically important, and we as leaders must pay attention to our ability to maintain focus and keep going. Workers as well as learners need breaks, exercise, energizing activities, and proper food. Plan to incorporate the ideas outlined here throughout your training.

Prepare to use this activity at some point in your program, but keep in mind that it needs to be used when you realize that people need energizing in order to go on.

Trainer's Notes for Activity 41

STEP-BY-STEP PROCEDURE

Step 1: Introduce the topic by saying,

"Our energy tends to ebb and flow when we're working on something wonderful or critically important. Leaders must be prepared to step in and reenergize their people.

"I have chosen this time to introduce this discussion because you look (overwhelmed, fatigued, tired) and need a break. So, first I want you to put your heads down while I dim the lights and play some quiet music. Take a short power nap."

Step 2: How can you help participants get reenergized? Ask them to stand in groups of four to five next to one of the flipcharts or a chart paper on the wall. Give each person a pad of sticky notes. Ask them to write down all of the ideas (one per note) they can think of that will help re-energize people who must work together for hours on end. They are to first write all of their ideas down, and then together try to group the ideas under similar categories.

While they are still standing, put on some lively music and lead the group in a few stretching exercises or dance movements (or get a volunteer who's adept at this to do it).

In the whole group, review the suggestions and merge ideas into similar groupings. Then have everyone take a piece of fruit for a snack and find a place to sit down.

Step 3: Share a few other ideas, such as these:

➜ Variety in activity and even location can help energy levels. No one can stay awake doing the same activity all the time, so prepare a sequence of tasks and topics that provide variety. For instance, combine discussion of a serious issue with something lighter or humorous. Or use part of a work session to solve a problem and another portion to evaluate how the group is working together.

➜ Regroup team members regularly. If you form sub-groups to work on a problem, be sure to mix people up once in a while. If they do not know one another, encourage them to sit with different people occasionally.

➜ Our metabolism dictates when we will have the most energy. Half of your group will be alert in the morning, a large number will perk up in the afternoon, and a small number will wish you could meet in the evening. Vary the time when you meet so you can draw on the energy of the group members.

➜ Also, vary where you meet. By meeting in different parts of a large organization, people get to see where their colleagues work. Try to occasionally meet in a setting away from work. Variety provides a fresh perspective.

➜ Research shows that people can sit still and concentrate for approximately forty-five minutes to one hour at a time. Take a break every hour so that people can go to the rest room, make a quick phone call, get a breath of fresh air, or network.

Provide for some physical exercise to re-energize the group. When they seem tired, do some yawning and stretching together. Have a set of easy exercises that can be done in your meeting room. Often there is someone in the group who would be glad to conduct these exercise breaks.

Schedule walks, even if it is only around the building. The whole group could walk together. Sometimes pair people up and give them something to talk about while they take a ten-minute walk.

→ Food and beverages can help a meeting; however, the wrong ones will hinder it. Many people drink too much coffee because that is all that is available, but the extra caffeine tends to make them irritable and wired. So, if there are to be beverages, provide a variety: tea (including herbal), coffee, diet and regular soft drinks, juices, mineral water, and milk. The same holds true with food: The traditional donut or danish has so much sugar that it leaves people with a quick high and then a drop in energy. Select breads or muffins with less sugar, and provide yogurt or fruit; you'll find your team members sustaining their energy longer.

This is also true of snacks. Keep that bowl of fruit available (or energy bars, nuts, etc.) throughout the session so those who need something can get it easily. If you all eat lunch together, try to pick a lighter menu or at least take time for a walk after the meal.

Step 4: Summarize what was presented, and ask each person to select 2–3 of the ideas and commit to use them in the next meeting they lead.

Call for a break!

POST-ACTIVITY REVIEW

Take time shortly after conducting this activity to reflect on how it went, how engaged the participants were, and what questions they raised. Then, make notes that include how much time you actually spent on the activity.

PART FOUR

Bring Out Their Best!

The activities in Part Four are designed to help leaders excel and perform at their best.

The first two activities show two different sides of an effective leader: the leader as a coach and the leader as a teacher. *Listen Up! The Leader as Coach* and *Pass It On! The Leader as Teacher* are both good ways to explore these very important roles in isolation.

Taking a risk that has been carefully planned is sometimes appropriate and even necessary, but too many of us are scared to take any kind of risk. The activity *Dare to Take Risks* should help you handle this dilemma.

Successful leaders do have mentors, usually more than one in a career. The next activity outlines how to assess what we need and want in a mentor and provides suggestions on how to find the right one.

Creativity is another hallmark of a good leader. The activity *Searching for Creativity* touches on some of the ways to add this skill to your toolbox. But being able to fill several flipcharts with great ideas isn't enough; you have to put a few of those fabulous suggestions to the test. *The Alphabet Poem* shows you how to apply creativity.

The next two activities, *Leadership Stations: Your Final Journey* and *Dear Diary* suggest creative ways to assess what participants have learned about leadership as they develop their career-development plans.

We wanted to conclude on a positive note, so we are closing with two upbeat activities that can be used at the end of a leadership workshop or program: *Keep the Flame Burning: Recognizing Others* and *Add Heart to Your Workplace Celebrations.* We hope they are all helpful, energizing, and effective as you continue your efforts to become and develop good leaders.

42

LISTEN UP!
The Leader as Coach

Overview of Activity

Coaching employees is a necessary business competency for leaders. This exercise offers leaders realistic and helpful suggestions.

Objectives

→ To identify the importance of coaching employees.
→ To review coaching styles.

Setting Up the Activity

GROUP SIZE
Up to 20 participants

ESTIMATED TIME
2 hours

TRAINING METHODS
→ Coaching
→ Discussion (large- and small-group)
→ Case study
→ Journal writing
→ Hands-on art activity

MATERIALS

→ Handout 42.1: *Finding the Milestones in Your Career Life*

→ Handout 42.2: *Coaching Styles*

→ Handout 42.3: *Dealing with Challenging Coaching Situations*

→ Handout 42.4: *Case Study Scenarios* (one copy per group or one per participant)

→ Handout 42.5: *Coaching an Employee*

EQUIPMENT AND SUPPLIES

→ Colored paper

→ Flipchart and markers

→ Self-sticking notes

ROOM SET-UP

→ Open space (for flying paper airplanes)

→ Tables and chairs for small groups

Comments

Savvy leaders coach employees so that they can improve their skills and develop greater self-confidence. Participants will have had good and bad experiences being coached and should draw on these experiences in order to evaluate their own coaching style.

This activity ties in well with Activity 32 on style flexing, so consider presenting them in sequence. To be an effective coach, you absolutely MUST be flexible.

RESOURCES

The scenarios in this activity were inspired by *The Practical Coach,* a video available from Media Partner Corporation (1-800-408-5657).

Trainer's Notes for Activity 42

STEP-BY-STEP PROCEDURE

Step 1: Introduce the activity by telling participants:

"We will begin with a variety of activities that will provide you with insights into how to coach other people. You will learn how to apply coaching techniques to different situations."

Now give directions for making paper airplanes: "I am handing out sheets of colored paper to each person. Use the paper to make a paper airplane that will fly." Allow several minutes so participants can experiment with different construction techniques.

Step 2: When everyone is done, line people up along one side of the room. Ask them to wait for the signal, and then fly their airplane, letting it stay where it lands. Note which airplane flew the farthest, and ask that person to coach the rest of the participants on how to design and construct a plane based on this successful model.

Step 3: Pass out more paper and allow several minutes for instruction and new construction.

Step 4: Line everyone up again and comment on the results. Resume the competition.

Step 5: Debrief the activity, and discuss how the results changed after some coaching.

Step 6: Divide the group into pairs, and ask the pairs to take five minutes to identify the roles a coach might have to take on with an employee.

Talk about what the pairs came up with, and put these ideas on the flipchart.

Ask for definitions of coaching, and see if people can come to quick agreement on a good one.

Step 7: Distribute Handout 42.1, *Finding the Milestones in Your Career Life,* and provide these instructions:

"On the grid, place sticky notes on years where you experienced some kind of high point in your career development. They will be your milestone markers."

If you had a coach who helped you with this achievement, add his/her name.

Now write a journal entry, answering these questions:

➔ Now that you have identified major milestones in your career, how important was coaching to your career growth and success?

➔ What kind of coach best meets your needs?

Step 8: Now it's time to look at how coaching styles differ from one another. Distribute Handout 42.2, *Coaching Style,* and go over the advantages and disadvantages of these styles:

Directive coaching style
Nondirective coaching style

Ask participants to turn to their journals and write about the kind of coach who best serves their needs.

Step 9: Present and encourage discussion about communication strategies for coaching. Use these questions:

What communication barriers will hinder your coaching success?

Which of your communication abilities will enhance your coaching success?

Step 10: In this 30-minute exercise, you will cover how to deal with coaching problems.

Distribute and review the Two-Minute Challenge on Handout 42.3, *Dealing with Challenging Coaching Situation,*

Then divide participants into groups of three.

Ask one person to be the Leader/Coach, the second to be the Employee, and the third to be a Process Observer.
    Distribute Handout 42.4, *Case Study Scenarios.* to each group. Participants will assume their roles and follow the script, which will outline several ways to handle the situation. Ask each Process Observer to give feedback on how each Leader/Coach handled the situation. The Employee must also share his/her reaction to the different approach taken for each problem.

Step 11: Give participants some time to practice giving specific and positive feedback in their small groups.
    Then ask people to switch roles while you distribute the second scenario to each group. Then have them begin acting out their roles, using the script that outlines several ways to handle the situation. Ask each Process Observer to give feedback on how each Leader/ Coach handled the situation. The Employee should also share his/her reaction to the different approach to each problem. Wind things up by distributing copies of Handout 42.5, *Coaching an Employee,* for use with employees.

POST-ACTIVITY REVIEW

Take time shortly after conducting this activity to reflect on how it went, how engaged the participants were, and what questions they raised. Then, make notes that include how much time you actually spent on the activity.

Finding the Milestones in Your Career Life

On the chart below record the key milestones in your career. Write the event and the name of anyone who might have served as a coach to help you accomplish that event in the square. Use abbreviations if you need to. Be sure to follow the "importance scale" on the left of the chart.

Level of
Importance:

10									
9									
8									
7									
6									
5									
4									
3									
2									
1									
0 Your Age	15	20	25	30	35	40	45	50	55

Coaching Styles

Choose the coaching style that fits best for:

→ person being coached.
→ Your own personal style.
→ The situation.
→ The outcomes you desire.

The two main kinds of coaching are:

Directive coaching
Nondirective coaching.

The advantages and disadvantages of each style are described on the next two pages.

Directive Coaching
In directive coaching, the coach takes the position of expert: He or she tells the coachee what needs to be done and how to do it.

Advantages

→ It saves time.
→ It allows the coachee to see a model of what worked in another situation.
→ It provides a framework for clear expectations of the outcomes.

Disadvantages

→ It tends to set up a parent-child communication pattern.
→ It might not address the needs of the individual.
→ It can inhibit creativity and close off communication.

Language examples of directive coaching

"Let me show you how to do that."
"Don't do it that way. This method works better."
"You shouldn't . . . ."

COACHING STYLES (continued)

Nondirective Coaching

In nondirective coaching, the coach and the coachee create a partnership to solve problems or develop skills. The coach takes the position of a facilitator to accomplish the outcomes. The coachee decides on the appropriate goal.

Advantages

It addresses the needs and desires of the coachee.

It doesn't require that the coach be an expert on the content.

It doesn't require as much up-front preparation.

Disadvantages

It requires the coach to be an excellent listener and facilitator.

It tends to require a longer commitment of coaching time.

It puts more emphasis on the coachee's willingness to commit to change and carry through.

Language examples of non-directive coaching

"What do you think the problem is?"

"How often does this happen?"

"If you tried this again, what would you do differently?"

"What matters most to you?"

"What would you like to achieve?"

"What have you tried so far?"

"How do you know that this is true?"

"Who might be able to help?"

"What support do you need?"

"What options do you think are best?"

"What might get in the way?"

Dealing with Challenging Coaching Situations

There are three basic rules every coach should follow:

1. Never let great work go unnoticed.
   When you see it, say it.

2. Never let poor work go unnoticed.
   Make your comments privately, but be positive.

3. Use the two-minute challenge:
   State what you have observed.
   Wait for a response.
   Remind them of the goal.
   Ask for a specific solution.
   Agree together on a solution that both of you can accept.

Case Study Scenarios

TWO "PROBLEM" COACHING SITUATIONS

Problem #1: Elaine helps out

One of the staff members in marketing is out sick, and a big project must get out the door by day's end. Elaine comes in from another area to help out. She has a great attitude. She worked hard all day, and here she is staying late to meet the deadline.
As she leaves,

> First try: Manager says: "Good night Elaine," but gives no detailed feedback on Elaine's efforts to get the project out on time.

> Second try: Manager says, "Thanks Elaine. You were a big help."

> Third try: Manager says, "I really appreciate the way you were willing to put your own work aside for a whole day to help us out. You have great organizational skills, and they were just what we needed to get this project finished." The manager provides some specific examples of what she means.

Problem #2: Correcting Eileen's bad work

Eileen is overheard to loudly say, "Well, I am sorry you feel that way." She then slams down the phone as the manager walks by.

> First try: In front of other workers, the manager says, "I hope you aren't talking to all of our customers that way. If you can't stay in control, you'd better take a break."

> Second try: "Sounds like someone was really giving you a rough time there. Why don't you take a break with me for a few minutes? (Walk out together) Can I be of any help?"

> Third try: Manager says, "Eileen, you provide great service to our customers. I know that for certain. What could you have done differently with this one?"

Coaching an Employee

Employee's name: —————————————————————————————

I would like to meet with you to discuss some of the following items on ———— ————————————————— . Your ideas and input are important to me. Please take time to think over your responses before our meeting.

1. What do you believe is the most challenging part of your work?

2. Do you feel appreciated?

3. What motivates you to do a good job?

4. What are the greatest obstacles to getting your work done?

5. What resources do you need that you don't currently have?

6. What do you like best about your job? Least?

7. What do you believe are your strengths?

8. What areas would you like to improve?

9. What can I do to make your job less frustrating and more satisfying?

10. What career goals would you like to be working toward?

43

PASS IT ON!

The Leader as Teacher

Overview of Activity

Leaders often have to help their staffs with learning development plans. This activity identifies ways that the leader can teach in an active, impactful way.

Objectives

→ To review participant experiences in learning situations.
→ To demonstrate how a learning plan can be put together.
→ To develop and implement one learning plan with employees.

Setting Up the Activity

GROUP SIZE
Up to 20 participants divided into groups of 4 to 5

ESTIMATED TIME
45 minutes

TRAINING METHODS
→ Discussion
→ Presentation
→ Writing

MATERIALS
Handout 43.1: *Creating Exemplary Learning Experiences*

EQUIPMENT AND SUPPLIES
None

ROOM SET-UP
Tables and chairs

Comments

It is important to encourage people to continuously teach others what they have learned. When we teach others, we reinforce what we also have learned. We become role models, encouraging employees to pass on what they learn, as well.

Ideally, this activity should be conducted after participants have gone through most of the leadership program. They will be able to select a module they know they can adapt for implementation with their own employees and develop a learning plan. If possible, do this module when there is time to implement these plans and report back the results at a subsequent workshop.

Trainer's Notes for Activity 43

STEP-BY-STEP PROCEDURE

Step 1: Introduce the activity by saying:

"There is no better way to demonstrate your confidence in your employees than to take time on a regular basis to teach them things that you are learning. It will build their skills and help you crystallize your thinking on any topic. For this reason, we suggest that you choose a time each month to provide a short training session with some group in your company."

Step 2: Ask participants to describe a time when they knew they weren't learning much. Perhaps it was because . . .

- The presentation was boring.
- There were no breaks.
- The material was unrelated to their work.
- There was no variety.

Step 3: Hold a general discussion on the problems.

Now reverse the discussion topic and talk about times when their learning was meaningful. Perhaps it was because . . .

- The learning was "active."
- The material was relevant.
- The timing was right.

Step 4: Hold a general discussion on what people do right.

Distribute and review the Handout 43.1, *Creating Exemplary Learning Experiences.* Then divide the participants into groups of 4–6. Ask each group to choose one of the modules they attended during this leadership program that they would like to offer to their employees. Using the points on the handout, ask participants to develop a learning plan. Allow plenty of time for this activity.

Step 5: Give them this assignment: "Now conduct the learning module your group has developed with a few of your employees, and be prepared to report back the results to this group."

Step 6: Wrap up by reviewing the main points you discussed.

POST-ACTIVITY REVIEW

Take time shortly after conducting this activity to reflect on how it went, how engaged the participants were, and what questions they raised. Then, make notes that include how much time you actually spent on the activity.

Creating Exemplary Learning Experiences

The following nine suggestions come from the experiences of veteran trainers:

1. Plan ahead. Let your people know ahead of time just when, where, and why you will be calling them together. Entice them by stating a common problem or dilemma in the memo that you believe the session will help them solve.

2. Set expectations. Let everyone know that for this set period of time, you will be guiding them through a learning experience. Arrange for use of a training room, or schedule a location that is not used for staff meetings and other functions.

3. Organize your material. Grab their attention in the very beginning. Involve them in the topic by posing a leading question or telling a brief story.

    Plan the content. Divide the information you want to share into four or five main points (fewer or more, depending on the time). Since we know that people learn differently, each of these points will need to be illustrated with facts and figures, the bottom line, a story or example involving people, or some activity that involves the learner directly (writing, dialogue, small-group discussion, role play, etc.).

4. Use visuals. Many people learn best when there are colorful posters, flipcharts, handouts, or props that add interest and impact to their learning.

5. Plan for breaks. Educators have found that adult learners need a break about every 50 minutes. The break doesn't have to be more than 7–10 minutes to be effective.

6. Review the main concepts. Give participants a little quiz or an activity so they can use the material right away.

7. Make an impact at the end. Let people know how they can apply this new skill to their workplace. Hold individuals accountable for using this new skill as soon as possible. To reinforce the learning, check in from time to time to see how the skill is being used.

8. Provide snacks. It is always a nice gesture to have healthy beverages and some healthy snack available for the breaks. It renews energy and keeps people concentrating on the content.

9. Have fun! In this kind of exercise, you are demonstrating the importance of on-going workplace learning. Encourage others to share what they learn and what they can do.

44

DARE TO TAKE RISKS

Overview of Activity

Risking, de-risking, and evaluating the consequences of risks are all critical to understanding and analyzing risk as a critical leadership competency. This activity takes the leader step-by-step through a useful process.

Objectives

→ To engage participants in lively discussion about the kinds and levels of risk.

→ To identify each person's risk profile.

→ To create an awareness that what is risky for one person might be easy for another.

→ To explore the ways that women and men each approach and handle risk.

Setting Up the Activity

GROUP SIZE
Up to 20 participants

ESTIMATED TIME
1 1/2–2 hours

MATERIALS

→ Handout 44.1: *Evaluating a Risk*

→ Handout 44.2: *A Risk Evaluation Plan*

→ Prepared index cards for Step 1 (See Job Aid 44.1: *Risk-Taking Scenarios*)

TRAINING METHODS

→ Presentation

→ Discussion

→ Writing

→ Storytelling

EQUIPMENT AND SUPPLIES

→ Flipchart

→ Markers

ROOM SET-UP

Arrange tables in a square with the chairs on the outside so they will see one another during discussions. If possible, place two people at each table so they will already be arranged when you need them in pairs.

Comments

Being able to take risks and evaluating whether the consequences are worth the risk is a critical leadership skill. We face many different kinds of risks in business, and experience tells us that many risks can be mitigated or made less difficult and less dangerous. The exercises in this activity are designed to stimulate thinking and open up a dialogue as to what risks are most appropriate in their specific work circumstances.

If there is a time constraint, delete some of the sections of the activity; it is carefully divided to accommodate that. In Step 2, you can prepare a flipchart sheet ahead of time so you have some of the answers ready to share. An additional way to deepen response to this activity is to ask the participants to come to the training with an example of a business risk, for use in Step 7.

Trainer's Notes for Activity 44

STEP-BY-STEP PROCEDURE

Step 1: Introduce this topic of risk taking by setting up the scenario. Use Job Aid 44.1, *Risk-Taking Scenarios*. Also have it written on index cards, one card for each step):

To raise one million dollars for the charity of your choice.

→ Would you walk on a tightrope stretched between the 18th floor of the Amoco Building and the Republic Plaza Building? (Use an example of tall buildings in your own city and discuss responses.)

→ What if the money went to you personally? (Elicit response.)

→ What if the tightrope had a safety net 18 floors below? (Elicit response.)

→ What if, in addition to the safety net, the tightrope was actually a 6-inch wide plank? (Elicit response.)

→ If (in addition to the safety net and the 6-inch plank) a harness was also attached so you would only fall several feet before the harness stopped you, would you take the risk for $1,000,000? (Elicit response.)

→ Would you take the risk if, in addition to all of the above, one of the flying Wallendas held your hand during your walk? (Elicit response.)

Conclude by saying, "These are all levels of risks. I will ask you to think about whether or not some risks look more do-able if changes can be made. Risk is like that. If you don't take it, you will never feel the natural high you get from its successful conclusion!"

Step 2: Ask participants what the word "risk" means to them. Write answers on the flipchart.

Possible answers might include:

→ You take action despite the likelihood that there will be consequences of your decision or behavior.

→ When you do something that has an uncertain outcome, you are taking a risk.

→ Some risks are big, others are small.

→ Some risks bring reward and recognition, while others lead to failure and frustration.

→ Risks can be positive or negative.

All risks have at least one thing in common: They teach you about yourself and what you need to succeed in life/work, and that is very important if you want to move up.

Pose the following questions for discussion:

How does risk relate to your comfort zone?
How can we expand our risk potential?
Why don't we take more risks? Be sure participants make these points.

→ People aren't comfortable taking them.
→ They fear failure.
→ They can't take the first step.
→ Others might resent their decisions.

Step 3: Distribute Handout 44.1, *Evaluating a Risk.* Then talk about the notion of high-level, mid-level, and low-level risk. Ask participants to write an example of a risk they've taken (at each level) on the handout.

Explain that you are focusing on business risks. "Using a business context, think of a time when you stood up for something you felt really strongly about. Your motivation might have been to protect or defend yourself, another person, a belief you hold, or the organization itself. When you stand up for something, you are taking a risk—often a personal risk, whether it plays out physically, financially, or emotionally. Important: Risks are only taken when something powerful compels them."

When participants have completed all 13 questions, ask volunteers to share any special strategies they used.

Then ask, " What are the benefits of risk-taking?" Elicit responses such as these:

→ You learn to set stretching goals.

→ Goal-setting helps people solve problems, instead of placing blame.

→ Goal-setting means careful planning; this contributes to taking risks confidently.

→ When you set goals, you are able to improve on previous accomplishments.

→ You explore new opportunities.

→ You learn about yourself.

→ Your success with the risk enhances your confidence and determination.

Step 4: Explain what is probably obvious to all of you:

People perceive risks differently. Discuss these areas of difference:

→ One-person thinks it is risky to drive; another thinks it is riskier to fly.
→ Some people are not afraid to go rock climbing or skiing.
→ People have different attitudes about investing money.

Step 5: Tell participants that there are some risks each of us wants to take, but something holds us back. This is what we will focus on next.

Divide the group into pairs and distribute Handout 44.2, *A Risk Evaluation Plan.*

Ask each pair to work through the questions on the handout after they each identify something they want to do. (One person talks and the second takes notes.) After 10 minutes, tell them to reverse roles for another ten minutes.

Then direct pairs to ask of one another:

→ What are you afraid of in terms of taking this action, and how can you overcome these fears?

→ How can you use your knowledge and past experiences to deal with this risk?

→ What kinds of risks can you handle best?

→ Is there any preparation that you can take that will make it less risky?

→ What additional strategies can overcome barriers to achieving the desired results?

→ How can we, in this small group, be both a support group and a brainstorming group for risk? And why would this be helpful?

Step 6: Discuss with the total group how men and women have different attitudes toward risk-taking.

Tell the group:

Many women say that they are not particularly comfortable taking risks. However, men say that taking the risk and standing up for something you really believe in is incredibly powerful and energizing.

If you are well-prepared to argue for what you believe in—and if you don't totally lose control and you can keep the issue from getting personal—you will be respected for the confrontation. Remember, men might be "programmed" to expect and take risks, but everyone should understand that business is business. It is NOT personal! A man or woman who is not willing to take some risk will be at a career disadvantage. Many HR professionals say that the barriers to risk-taking in women are frequently internal, rather than external. Women find themselves taking criticism personally. Men and women should speak up in meetings if they have something worth saying. There might be some social discomfort (risk) in doing so, but it can be overcome.

Did you ever hear of the Imposter Syndromes? Some people do not evaluate themselves objectively; they are afraid that someone will really find out that they are not as bright or as competent or as . . . (you fill it in). This might surprise you, but some people in top positions still wonder exactly what they are doing and how they got there.

"If you are approached to take on a new project or position, think seriously about taking it. You wouldn't have been offered the project if someone didn't think you could handle it." Then continue: "Mind you, I am not suggesting that you throw caution to the wind. Being ambitious does not mean taking big risks. It means setting a stretch aspiration, and then using the tools and resources to de-risk that ambition."

What does a stretch aspiration look like for you?

What is the level of risk, after you de-risk it?

"You can learn to take more risks by getting more adept at evaluating them. Many companies equate innovation and growth with risk-taking. Certainly calculated risks must be taken, but getting to the future first is not simply a matter of having more risk-takers. Getting to the future first is less about making heroic investments than it is about de-risking heroic ambitions."

Step 7: Bring the session to a close:

"You have your plan for taking a risk, so try it out. Call your partner to let him/her know how it went. Then try to meet to again to review the questions on the handout. Be one another's support system. And good luck!"

POST-ACTIVITY REVIEW

Take time shortly after conducting this activity to reflect on how it went, how engaged the participants were, and what questions they raised. Then, make notes that include how much time you actually spent on the activity.

Evaluating a Risk

1. What risk did I take?

2. How was this risk consistent with my values?

3. Was I being pressured to take this risk?

4. What other choices did I have?

5. What effect did this have on my present and future status?

6. What feelings drove me to take that risk?

7. After taking the risk, what happened?

8. How/what changed?

9. How did others change?

10. In what ways was my organization (or I) better off from having taken this action?

11. How do I feel about myself after taking this risk?

12. What did I learn from taking this risk?

After completing this evaluation, I learned that risk _____

A Risk Evaluation Plan

The risk is:
1. How is this risk consistent with my values?
2. Am I being pressured to take this risk? (If so, by whom and for what reasons?)
3. What other choices do I have?
4. What effect(s) will taking this risk have on my future?
5. What will happen if I do not take this risk?
6. What feelings are driving me to take this risk?
7. After taking the risk, what do I think will happen?
8. How or what do I think will change?
9. How or what effects will there be on others?
10. In what ways do I think that my organization or I will be better off from having taken this risk?
11. How do I think I'll feel about myself after taking this risk?
12. After completing this list of questions, I learned (about the risk) that _____

After taking the risk, answer these questions:
1. After taking the risk, what did happen?
2. How or what changed, as a result of the risk?
3. In what ways are you or your organization better off from having taken this risk?
4. How do you feel about yourself after taking this risk?
5. What did you learn from participating in this risk that you can use in other contexts?
6. After completing this review checklist, I now understand that

_____

Risk-Taking Scenarios

To raise one million dollars for the charity of your choice:

→ Would you walk on a tightrope stretched between the 18th floor of the Amoco Building and the Republic Plaza Building?"(Use an example of tall buildings in your own city and discuss responses.)

→ "What if the money went to you personally?" (Elicit response.)

→ "What if the tightrope had a safety net 18 floors below?"(Elicit response.)

→ "What if, in addition to the safety net, the tightrope was actually a 6-inch wide plank?" (Elicit response.)

→ "If (in addition to the safety net and the 6-inch plank) a harness was also attached so you would only fall several feet before the harness stopped you, would you take the risk for $1,000,000?" (Elicit response.)

→ "Would you take the risk if, in addition to all of the above, one of the flying Wallendas held your hand during your walk?" (Elicit response.)

SUCCESSFUL LEADERS HAVE MENTORS

Overview of Activity

The roles of mentor and protégé are explored in this hands-on module. Multiple handouts also guide the leader.

Objectives

→ To understand the roles and responsibilities of mentors and protégés.
→ To clarify the steps necessary to find and work with a mentor.

Setting Up the Activity

GROUP SIZE
Up to 20 participants

ESTIMATED TIME
45 minutes

TRAINING METHODS
→ Discussion
→ Storytelling
→ Assessment
→ Hands-on art project

MATERIALS
→ Handout 45.1: *Are You Ready to Be a Protégé?*

→ Handout 45.2: *Roles and Responsibilities of Protégés and Mentors*
→ Handout 45.3: *A Plan for Finding a Mentor*

EQUIPMENT AND SUPPLIES
Posters of well-known leaders (men and women)
Skeletal outline of the human body

ROOM SET-UP
Tables and chairs arranged in a semicircle

Comments

Most successful leaders benefited from having a mentor. Some participants might have had someone who influenced them or provided coaching. Some will say their mentor was their boss. In this exercise, accept whatever experiences they have had and encourage them to review those experiences as you present this model of mentors.

VARIATION
One way to vary the finding-a-mentor exercise is to turn it into a creative art project. Each person needs a large and clear space at a table. Give each person poster board and a skeletal outline of a human body. Place a pile of craft sticks (i.e., popsicle sticks) and glue sticks near each person.

Step by step (as outlined in Handout 45.3, A *Plan for Finding a Mentor*), participants add sticks to their mentor's "body."

1. Three professional goals on sticks are glued on the body's trunk.
2. Desired characteristics are glued on each finger of the left hand.
3. Additional preferences are glued on each finger of the right hand.
4. The names of places to look for a mentor are glued on the left foot.
5. The name of possible mentors are glued on the right foot.

Participants should help one another identify barriers to pursuing these plans and suggest potential mentors.

This graphic representation can be posted by participants in a place where they will be visually reminded of their plan to get a mentor.

Trainer's Notes for Activity 45

STEP-BY-STEP PROCEDURE

Step 1: Introduce the activity by clarifying the difference between a mentor and a protégé:

A Mentor facilitates the personal and professional growth of an individual by sharing the knowledge and insights that have been learned through the years. The mentor sees the potential in a less-experienced person, and helps to guide that individual along a professional path. The mentor serves as the protégé's role model and champion.

A Protégé is an achiever groomed for advancement: He or she is provided with opportunities to excel beyond the limits of her/his position.

Identify the importance of having a mentor by pointing out successful leaders who have publicly acknowledged their mentors. Tell your own story of having a mentor.

Step 2: Talk about other examples of leaders and their mentors and the benefits that come from having a model. Refer to the posters. Ask participants about their own mentors. Then ask whether anyone has had a career mentor.

Possible benefits:

→ You can move forward faster.

→ You will definitely increase your network.

→ You might have the opportunity to work on challenging and interesting projects.

→ You will have a smoother transition into unfamiliar territory.

→ Your credibility is increased because of your association with your mentor.

→ You might gain a good colleague or friend.

→ You can learn how to be a mentor.

→ You can expand your generosity.

Step 3: Distribute Handouts 45.1, *Are You Ready to Be a Protégé?*, and 45.2, *Roles and Responsibilities of Protégés and Mentors.* Discuss the roles and responsibilities of a protégé. Use the Handout 45.2. Then ask participants to complete Handout 45.1 before the next step.

Step 4: Distribute Handout 45.3, *A Plan for Finding a Mentor,* and go over seven steps in the process:

1. Identify what you need (privately).

2. Review the characteristics most frequently found in mentors and rank their importance to you (privately).

3. Evaluate and select what you are looking for in a mentor. Have participants get into groups of 3 for this next step:

4. Create a list of potential mentors. One by one, each person explains what he or she is looking for in a mentor. The members of the group should help her/him identify some potential mentors.

    After each person has at least a short list of potential mentors, reassemble and open up the discussion to the total group. Ask anyone who is stuck trying to create a pool of candidates to summarize what she/he is looking for so that more suggestions can be gathered.

5. Participants should then apply their own list of criteria about what they want in a mentor to the list of potential mentors.

6. Now have participants form pairs to learn how to approach prospective mentors and sell yourself to these prospective mentors (Step #7). One person plays the role of the mentor, while the other practices how to approach a prospective mentor using the ideas on their handout. Then they switch roles. Each provides feedback on the approach used by the other person. Take a few minutes with the whole group to summarize what was learned.

Step 5: Review the items participants identified as being important to them in this kind of relationship. They should be made a part of the mentor-protégé agreement. Then draw up a sample agreement on the flipchart, using input from participants. Explain that they should have a draft proposal ready to discuss with their new mentor. Give them time to rough one out. Suggest that they put the final agreement in writing.

Step 6: End the session by sharing a few suggestions on how to handle the mentor-protégé relationship in case . . .

→ *My mentor wants to date me.*

The answer is "No!" Never date your mentor . . . not while you are in this relationship, at least. It will only backfire on one or both of you.

→ *My mentor is moving beyond our agreement, asking me to do personal errands for him such as getting his car washed.*

Be assertive and say no. Remind him of the boundaries of this relationship.

→ *My manager is envious of my relationship with the mentor.* Involve your manager in setting goals. Encourage your manager and your mentor to talk with one another about you and your professional plan.

→ *My peers are jealous.*

Talk with your mentor and manager to determine what you can do. Generously share what you are learning with your peers. Review with your jealous peers how they can find a mentor.

→ *Our personalities clash. We are really mismatched.*

Tactfully talk with your mentor about whether the relationship should be continued. You might need to end this relationship and go find another. Be sure to learn from this experience.

→ *My mentor won't let me go.*

Clarify whether or not you are really ready to move on. Talk with your mentor about your readiness to change the scope of your relationship. Point out your original goals in your agreement and indicate that you have achieved them.

POST-ACTIVITY REVIEW

Take time shortly after conducting this activity to reflect on how it went, how engaged the participants were, and what questions they raised. Then, make notes that include how much time you actually spent on the activity.

Are You Ready to Be a Protégé?

A Protégé is an achiever who is being groomed for advancement by being provided with opportunities to excel beyond the limits of his or her position.

Are you ready to be a protégé?
As you get ready to move into a relationship with a mentor, it is important to think about your own motivation, skills, and needs that you will bring to this experience. Ponder the following questions:

➔ What new experiences do you want to learn more about within your profession?

➔ What opportunities are you looking for that will help you advance in your profession?

➔ Do you have the drive and motivation to see this through to the end?

➔ Are you willing to be an active participant in this learning process?

➔ How much time are you willing to put into this process?

➔ What are the indicators of your potential to become successful at higher levels of leadership?

Am I ...	Agree	Neutral	Disagree
Am I a peak performer in my field?			
Am I striving to move up into new positions?			
Am I motivated for success?			
Am I assertive, and do I show initiative?			
Am I self-confident?			
Am I eager to learn?			
Am I a team player?			
Am I patient?			
Am I willing to give back to others?			
Am I generally positive about my work and people?			
Am I willing to listen and accept advice?			

ARE YOU READY TO BE A PROTÉGÉ? (continued)

Which of your career goals can a mentor help you achieve? Read over the characteristics often found in protégés to see which ones pertain to you. Decide if you agree, disagree, or are neutral:

If you agree with nine or more of the above questions, you should seriously consider a mentor relationship.

If you disagree or are neutral about three or more of these questions, you might need to re-evaluate your motives, your skills, your attitude, and your experiences. Show your self-evaluation to two people who know you well. You might find that they perceive you more favorably than you rate yourself.

The Roles and Responsibilities of Protégés and Mentors

Roles and Responsibilities of a Protégé

Now that you know you are ready to be a protégé, you will need to keep in mind the following guidelines about your role and responsibilities:

→ Be open to learning. Constructively listen to your mentor, and take his or her advice and counsel seriously.

→ Contact your mentor whenever you confront difficult situations, when you need advice, or when you are not sure of the right approach to a problem.

→ Seek out opportunities to take advantage of the mentoring relationship.

→ Keep your mentor apprised of your needs. Take the time to check in on a regular basis.

→ Be open to meet with your mentor whenever and wherever they suggest.

→ Give back. Pay attention to what your mentor might need from you, and be ready to provide appropriate assistance.

Roles and Responsibilities of a Mentor

→ Effectively challenge the protégé's inappropriate intentions or behaviors.

→ Help the protégé by listening or telling a story about how you solved a similar problem.

→ Work with the protégé to look for solutions to his or her professional dilemma.

→ Suggest books, tapes, or courses that will enhance the protégé's knowledge.

→ Let him or her shadow you and learn by watching.

→ "Walk the talk" so you model authenticity.

A Plan for Finding a Mentor

Follow these seven steps to locate and select a mentor:

Step 1: Identify what you need. Before you approach any prospects, determine your professional needs and identify your goals.

Step 2: Review the following common characteristics of mentors. Then rank their importance to you.

_____ They have a large circle of influence and a broad-based network.

_____ They are people-oriented.

_____ They know how to motivate others.

_____ They are effective teachers.

_____ They are secure in their position and profession.

_____ They are usually high achievers who set lofty career goals, continually evaluate these goals, and strive to reach them.

_____ They are able to give the protégé some visibility.

_____ They value their profession, their work, and public service.

_____ They respect others.

Step 3: Evaluate and select what you are looking for in a mentor:

➜ Do you want to work with a male mentor? A woman mentor?

➜ Do you want to work with a mentor from within your organization, or from outside it?

➜ Do you want to work with a mentor who is in your profession, or someone who is not?

A PLAN FOR FINDING A MENTOR (continued)

> → How important is it to you that the mentor models the type of behaviors you desire?
>
> → How important is it to you that the mentor has the knowledge and experience you wish to obtain?

Step 4: Create a list of potential mentors. Here are some ways some protégés add people to their list:

> → Identify people who "walk the talk."
>
> → Identify people you admire and respect.
>
> → Look at people you already know who can become your mentor.
>
> → Look through your rolodex, database, and membership lists.
>
> → Ask others who have had a mentor how they found theirs.
>
> → Check to see if your company has a mentoring program.
>
> → If there is no mentoring program, talk with your human resources department for suggestions.
>
> → Ask people who are knowledgeable in your field for suggestions.
>
> → Put out the word to your family and friends.

Step 5: Apply your list of criteria about what you want in a mentor to your list of potential mentors.

Step 6: Approach your prospective mentor(s). Here are some suggestions:

> → If you don't know the individual personally, determine who does. Speak to him/her about how to get an introduction. Then use it!

A PLAN FOR FINDING A MENTOR (continued)

➜ If the individual is only an acquaintance of yours, volunteer to do something with them on the same project or team.

➜ Invite the individual to breakfast or lunch.

➜ Ask if you can drive them to the airport or to an event an hour away.

➜ Attend an event in which the individual is involved, so you can engage in conversation.

Step 7: Sell yourself to these prospective mentors.

➜ Tell him/her what you admire about them. People love to be praised. Just be sincere.

➜ Outline what you think you need from a mentor.

46

SEARCHING FOR CREATIVITY

Overview of Activity

This module explores elements of creativity and ways to encourage the imaginative process.

Objectives

→ To understand how creativity and innovation impacts leaders.
→ To analyze what makes a company creative.
→ To examine some of the myths about creativity in corporations.
→ To study our own process of coming up with creative ideas.
→ To learn the differences between linear and creative thinking.
→ To try out processes for expanding thinking.

GROUP SIZE
Up to 20 participants

ESTIMATED TIME
3 hours

TRAINING METHODS
→ Discussion
→ Video
→ Small-group exercises
→ Presentation
→ Journal writing

MATERIALS

→ Handout 46.1: *My Own Creative Process*

→ Handout 46.2: *Elements of Creativity*

→ Handout 46.3: *Creative Techniques to Encourage Expanded Thinking*

EQUIPMENT AND SUPPLIES

→ VCR and monitor

→ FISH film

→ Flipchart and stand

→ Creative toys for participants to manipulate

→ Empty can and dried beans

→ Plastic fish

→ Thin and fat colored markers

→ Colored paper

→ White 3" x 5" index cards

→ Props that can be used for creative "product" ideas

ROOM SET-UP

Chairs facing flipcharts and VCR

Tables and chairs for small groups

Comments

In today's fast paced workplaces, employees need to solve problems and create innovations quickly and efficiently. The leader needs to know how to draw out the very best ideas and solutions from employees and team members. Therefore, this module stirs up their creative juices.

RESOURCES

A Whack on the Side of the Head. How You Can Be More Creative by Roger von Oech. New York: Warner Books, Inc., 1998.

The Creativity Tools Memory Jogger by Diane Ritter and Michael Brassard GOAL/QPC. 1998 available at www.goalqpc.com or call 978-685-6370

Trainer's Notes for Activity 46

STEP-BY-STEP PROCEDURE

Step 1: Introduce the topic by asking this question for the group to respond to: "Why should creativity and innovation be an important area of study for leaders?"

Answer:

– Creative thinking can give an organization a competitive advantage
– Creativity enhances and adds meaning to routine jobs

Ask participants what the difference is between creativity and innovation. After you get a few responses, share the following definitions on the flipchart:

→ Creativity is a process used to generate something new and potentially useful, without being directly shown or taught.

→ Creativity is a process that creates order out of chaos.

→ Innovation is the product or concept resulting from a creative idea.

Step 3: Then show the FISH film as a case study of a company with a creative vision. Ask viewers to write down the steps the company took to achieve their vision.

Ask, "What barriers do you see that leaders in your company erect that might prevent creativity from taking place?" Discuss this in pairs and have each pair put 3 to 4 brief responses on poster paper. Post and discuss as a group.

Step 4: Ask participants, "What does the process of creativity look like?" Ask them to think about an innovation they came up with. Distribute Handout 46.1, *My Own Creative Process,* and allow time for completion.

Step 5: Give each person seven white index cards. Tell them that they are to design the steps that they think are involved in a creative process, writing only one step on each card.

In groups of three, have participants compare notes and come to some consensus about what the steps should be.

Step 6: Ask participants if they know the difference between linear thinking and lateral thinking. Explain the difference, using these ideas:

→ The brain is not a creative mechanism. Its purpose is to organize information and sort "like" bits of knowledge.

→ Bits of information that we cannot connect to what we already know get lost.

→ Linear thinking is a step-by-step process. First we do *this,* second we do *that.* Where do we find examples of linear thinking?

➜ "Lateral thinking" was a term promoted by Edward DeBono to describe how we switch tracks and think about something in another way.

Humor is one example of the use of lateral thinking. Example: A man says to a woman: "If I were married to you, I would poison your coffee." The woman says to the man: "If I were married to you, I'd drink the coffee."

The writer Alex Osborn says that there are seven ways to look at a subject or product creatively. (SCAMPER is the mnemonic to remember.) Distribute Handout 46.2, *Elements of Creativity* and go over the seven elements. Use the examples below to get people started:

S = Substitute

C = Combine (VCR with the television, combined in one machine)

A = Adapt (wireless phones)

M = Modify or Magnify or add to (books on tape)

P = Put to another use (use a computer to watch a DVD movie)

E = Eliminate (Sony Walkman eliminated the ability to record)

R = Rearrange or Reverse (Alfred Sloan, CEO of General Motors, reversed the idea that people pay for the car before they drive it. He pioneered installment buying.)

After participants have had time to complete the handout, give them the following instructions so they can try out lateral thinking:

1. With a partner, create a new product or service.
2. Decide on the features or uses of the product.
3. Identify the benefits of the product.
4. Write a commercial to "sell" it.
5. What song would best suit this product or service?
6. Pitch your product to the group (have some props available for use).

Write out the instructions on a flipchart and allow time to select partners and proceed. Then debrief.

Step 7: Distribute Handout 46.3, *Creative Techniques to Encourage Expanded Thinking,* and take participants through each part of the process. If there is time, do one or both of the activities.

Step 8: Summarize what has been covered. Then allow participants to write out (either in a journal or in a notebook) what they can do to be more creative at work.

POST-ACTIVITY REVIEW

Take time shortly after conducting this activity to reflect on how it went, how engaged the participants were, and what questions they raised. Then, make notes that include how much time you actually spent on the activity.

My Own Creative Process

Take a couple of minutes to reach back into your past to a time when you came up with an innovation of your own—not necessarily something related to business. With that innovation in mind, answer the questions that follow:

The innovation I am thinking of is: _____

1. Did this innovation come about because there was a problem that you were trying to solve, or was this just a new way of approaching an issue?

2. Did this idea come to you because you were giving a lot of thought to this subject, or did it just pop into your head?

3. Was the problem solved by this idea?

4. How long did you think about this issue before the idea came to you?

5. What steps did you go through as you worked to come up with this new idea?

6. After you came up with the idea, what did you do to make it a reality? (Be specific.)

7. What have you learned about what you personally need to do in order to be at your creative best? Is there a time of day when you work best? Is there a place you go to do your best work? Do you work best alone, or with others?

Elements of Creativity

To think creatively, we need to be able to do these seven things with our ideas:

S = Substitute
C = Combine
A = Adapt
M = Modify or magnify
P = Put to another use
E = Eliminate
R = Rearrange or reverse

For example, the person who created the idea of producing an electronic device that combined a television and a VCR was putting two good ideas together to create another (combining).

Think of an example of each of the concepts contained in the SCAMPER mnemonic.

Substitute:

Combine:

Adapt:

Modify:

Put to another use:

Eliminate:

Rearrange:

Creative Techniques to Encourage Expanded Thinking

1. **The F.I.S.H.**

    This is a great activity to use with an ongoing team that quickly dismisses ideas as they come up.

    Give members of the team a piece of colored paper and a marker. Take turns coming up with common negative statements that put people or ideas down in a group discussion. Have different people write down these statements as the group comes up with them, and post the statements in the room where you normally work. At the same meeting, introduce a plastic fish. Tell the group that this fish eats Fatally Inappropriate Slimy Hits (abbreviation: F.I.S.H.) that destroy all ideas in their infancy. When you want to fish for new ideas, explain that the fish will be passed to anyone who attacks new ideas before they get a hearing.

    Here are a few common ego-bashing statements:

    "It will cost too much."   "That's unrealistic."
    "That's no fun."   "It's not in the budget."
    "You've got to be kidding!"   "We can't do that."
    "It doesn't make sense."   "We tried that before."

2. **Mind Mapping.**

    Mind mapping is a way to quickly record what you know so that you can make connections between two seemingly unrelated ideas and identify any gaps. Start with a question or problem that is challenging you. Put the problem or question in the middle of a blank page, using a symbol to represent the issue. Radiating out in all directions, put down brief thoughts about the topic, with pictures. This works just as well for a team as for individual problem-solving: If you want to use it as a team activity, have individuals undertake the process alone first. It is a way to get people to use their right brain, and provides a "method" for people to see in a creative way all of what they know about a problem or subject.

TECHNIQUES TO ENCOURAGE EXPANDED THINKING (continued)

3. **Spill the Beans.**

   This activity is a relaxed way to get people to put hidden agendas or difficult problems on the table that might be holding them back from making progress on a team project. Give each person a small can of baked beans, or bring in a used and washed bean can that you have filled with dried beans. Ask the group for a volunteer to "spill the beans" about some part of the project that is not going well. Go around the room, and encourage each person to follow suit. Issues that are brought up can be discussed one-by-one. (This process works best if it is handled by an unbiased facilitator.)

4. **Ideawriting 6-3-3.**

   This activity works well in groups of six or fewer. A topic or problem is stated at the top of a piece of paper, in question format. (The same question is stated in the same way on each person's form.) Each person is given three minutes to write three ideas across the top, creating three columns. When the time is up, the papers are passed to the person on the right. Each individual silently reads the idea in each column contributed by the person(s) before and adds more ideas in the appropriate columns, making a new row. The ideas can be an expansion of a previous idea, a variation of a previous idea, or something entirely new.

   When the papers have made it around the whole group, it is time to review the ideas and get rid of any duplicates. (This process can be undertaken at a later time by a committee or done by the last individual to have the paper.) Individuals are then asked to pull out interesting ideas from the paper in front of him/her and place them before the group. The group can then come to consensus on which ideas they should or would like to pursue further.

   Adapted with permission from *The Creativity Tools Memory Jogger* by Diane Ritter and Michael Brassard (pp. 21–30) GOAL/QPC. 1998 available at *www.goalqpc.com* or call 978-685-6370.

47

THE ALPHABET POEM
Practice Your Creativity

Overview of Activity

The leader can use this module to encourage greater creativity from his or her team.

Objectives

→ To stretch one's personal ability to be creative "on the spot."
→ To share differing points of view.
→ To encourage creativity in a group setting.

Setting Up the Activity

GROUP SIZE
Any number of participants

ESTIMATED TIME
Approximately 20 to 30 minutes (depending on the number of participants and the number of people who share their poems)

TRAINING METHODS
→ Presentation
→ Poetry writing
→ Group discussion

EQUIPMENT AND SUPPLIES
Pencil and paper for each participant

MATERIALS
None

ROOM SET-UP
Tables and chairs

Comments

Every good leader is able to use creativity to accomplish a goal, whether it be to solve a problem, find a solution, create a product, or energize a group of people. Creativity is a central competency of all leaders. This brief exercise is a fun way to stretch the imagination of the participants. It can be used in a variety of workshop designs.

Trainer's Notes for Activity 47

STEP-BY-STEP PROCEDURE

Step 1: Introduce the subject of poetry writing by asking participants to volunteer a favorite poem or poet. Discuss why people write or read poetry (ask those who do to share).

Explain that many people find it a good way to express feelings and ideas more creatively. Depending on how much interest there is in the subject, point out some common ways that new poets start. This can include rhyming couplets (e.g. Roses are red; violets are blue) or even descriptions of objects (where the whole focus is on a wonderfully evocative explanation of each sensory aspect of the object). Tell them that today's focus is on writing a poem to describe an event by using 26 words in alphabetical order, starting with an "a" word.

Again, by way of example:

All bad children definitely exhibit funky gross habits instead . . .

Step 2: The best way to ground this exercise so that you can have a discussion that pulls in everybody is to suggest a topic: Conflict, Power, Facilitating—whatever topic you are focusing on for the day. Then let them begin writing.

Step 3: After about ten or fifteen minutes of private writing, ask for volunteers to read their poems.

Step 4: Debrief. If discussion does not come naturally, ask such questions as:

What words or ideas came most naturally to you?
What was the most fun?

Step 5: Ask participants why they think some leaders use this exercise. Allow a few minutes for discussion.

POST-ACTIVITY REVIEW

Take time shortly after conducting this activity to reflect on how it went, how engaged the participants were, and what questions they raised. Then, make notes that include how much time you actually spent on the activity.

48

LEADERSHIP STATIONS
Your Final Journey

Overview of Activity

This is a good closure activity that encourages the participants to think about the next steps in their growth as leaders.

Objectives

→ To clarify participants' next steps in their personal and strategic career-development plan.

→ To use creativity and accelerated learning techniques to achieve what is often a cerebral exercise.

→ To encourage self-inquiry and evaluation in a non-threatening, enjoyable, "celebratory" setting.

Setting Up the Activity

GROUP SIZE
Up to 20 participants

ESTIMATED TIME
2 hours or more

TRAINING METHODS

→ Reflection   → Card-sort activity
→ Journal writing   → Visualization
→ Video presentation   → Round robin
→ Role play   → Hands-on art activity

MATERIALS

Copy Job Aid 48.1, *Description of the Leadership Stations,* and cut the paper so your have descriptions of all nine stations. Past each description on card stock paper. See Room Set-Up for where these 'signs' will be placed.

EQUIPMENT AND SUPPLIES

Review the descriptions of each "station." Then it will be clear what additional supplies and equipment will be needed.

→ Stacks of old magazines
→ Poster board
→ Glue sticks
→ Scissors
→ Blank music books (lined pages)
→ CD's of a variety of music
→ Clipboards (one per participant)
→ Blank paper
→ Pencils, pens
→ Colored markers
→ Timer
→ Projector screen
→ CD player

ROOM SET-UP

In advance: In the training space, create nine separate areas such as hallways or nooks. You need space to spread people out so that they have a feeling that there is some privacy when they are working at a station. Some leaders have created stations outdoors as well as in several separate rooms and say this set-up works quite well. Place a Station Sign at each of the nine station along with any necessary supplies or props.

Comments

This exercise can be done any time after the Leadership Development program begins. It is a good and creative way to re-energize the process of developing goals to achieve leadership competencies.

Consider total immersion in activities at nine separate "stations," in rotation. Have a second person available to help with the timer, so that participants can move from station to station with approximately equal time at each (10 minutes, with 20 minutes at the collage station). If other trainers are available, it is helpful at some of the stations to have a guide for the participants. Allow time at the end for some reporting back to the group.

The activity spreads out participants, so be sure that there is at least one person at every station. If the group is larger than nine, double-up at some stations. It will be clear which stations can handle this once you read the station descriptions.

This activity has also been used successfully to close leadership development programs.

Trainer's Notes for Activity 48

STEP-BY-STEP PROCEDURE

Step 1: Introduce the activity by explaining how important it is for individuals to clarify the next steps in their career by creating a personal- and strategic-development plan.

Tell everyone that they are about to experience a creative way to reflect on what they have learned in the program, as well as identify areas for future development.

Promise them that they will enjoy this journey, laugh, and celebrate while they learn concrete information about themselves.

Step 2: Give instructions for the activity as follows:

"You will visit nine stations, spending 10 minutes at each (except at the Collage station, where you will spend double-time). The instructions will be available at each station or the facilitator of the station will provide them for you.

Once everyone has visited all nine stations and completed the exercise, we expect you to provide one or two highlights for the rest of us to hear. Happy travels!"

Keep track of time, and signal when it is time for everyone to move to a new station.

Step 3: When everyone has completed the activity, get the group together and give them a few minutes to sort through their notes from all nine stations. Allow time for them to provide one or two highlights for the rest of the group to hear.

Then ask for feedback on this activity: How did the variety of activities enhance the experience? Which ones were the best? Worst? Encourage discussion about what they derived from the activity.

Step 4: Congratulate each participant on the efforts they are making to become the very best leaders they can. Try to say something positive about each person's accomplishment or performance in terms of the leadership competencies you have focused on.

POST-ACTIVITY REVIEW

Take time shortly after conducting this activity to reflect on how it went, how engaged the participants were, and what questions they raised. Then, make notes that include how much time you actually spent on the activity.

Description of the Leadership Stations

Station 1: Writing Your Celebration Song

If your leadership plan for the next three to six months is completed, you will want to celebrate. How and when will you celebrate?

Choose a tune you know well, and write some new words so you will have a song that spells out all the ways you plan to reward yourself for your accomplishments.

Station 2: Business Processes

What business processes do you believe you have mastered? Which business processes will you place on your Action Plan? Write these down.

What date will you choose to set for yourself to learn and understand this process? Add this to your ideas from the previous question.

Who will support you in learning these processes? Write the names of the people you want to cheer you on.

Station 3: Famous Character Role Play (of a coach or mentor)

Imagine yourself as a famous character from a book, movie, or TV who could be your favorite coach or mentor.

In their voice, what are the qualities and characteristics that you are looking for in your next coach or mentor?

In character, describe the qualities or characteristics, and be creative! Practice and be prepared to act out your character for us.

Station 4: Core Competencies (Use the competency deck prepared for Activity 19)

Review these cards, and sort them into three piles:

First pile: Which core competencies have you mastered and are using to sell yourself?

Second pile: Which core competencies need the most development?

DESCRIPTION OF THE LEADERSHIP STATIONS (continued)

Third pile: Which core competencies are well underway, but are not yet mastered?

Prioritize the top 3 competencies you plan to develop or improve next year.

Station 5: Collage of Strategic Goals

Using magazines, cut out pictures to make a collage that represents your long-term strategic goals—those that will require three to five years to accomplish. Make sure you write the goals in your Leadership Development Plan.

Station 6: Metaphor of Your Personal Vision, Mission, and Values

Use a metaphor that represents your vision, mission, and values. (Example: "I am an eagle. I fly high, alone, and unafraid. My instincts are strong, and I. . . ." or "I see a network—a web of connections. I am part of all things. I am a source of portions of this web, and I receive the support from these web connections. I am linked to. . . .")

Station 7: Marketing Plan: Promote Your Leadership!

What concrete steps do you plan to take immediately (over the next 3–6 months) to enhance your visibility? What are your strategic or long-term steps, beyond one year? Write these out.

Station 8: Poem: How do I position myself as a unique individual?

Write a poem or use prose to articulate how you are special and unique. "A is for action, B is for brain, C is for courage, D is for determination. . . ." or "I am fond of the color red. I always say what needs to be said. . . ."

Station 9: Visualize a "movie moment."

What are your key measures for career success? Visualize a movie scene in which you accomplish a career goal. If a trainer is available, he/she can write down the key measures from your creative musings, or you can jot down quick notes as you think.

49

KEEP THE FLAME BURNING

Recognizing Others

Overview of Activity

A leader must learn as many ways as possible to value the contributions of others. This is an essential part of motivation for high performance. Through role play, this module offers an opportunity to practice.

Objectives

→ To identify how people are motivated to work at their best.
→ To explore a variety of ways to reward and recognize others.

Setting Up the Activity

GROUP SIZE
Up to 20 participants

ESTIMATED TIME
30 to 45 minutes

TRAINING METHODS
→ Presentation
→ Role play

MATERIALS
→ Handout 49.1: *Role Play Cards*
→ Handout 49.2: *Keep the Flame Burning–Recognizing Others*

ROOM SET-UP
Chairs arranged in a circle

Comments

"Encouraging the Heart" is one of five dimensions thought by James Kouzes and Barry Posner to be characteristic of all effective leaders. There are many books and journal articles available that address the subject of employee recognition. This activity can act as an introduction to the subject of valuing and rewarding effort and performance.

RESOURCE
Encouraging the Heart by James Kouzes and Barry Posner (San Francisco: Jossey-Bass) 2003.

Trainer's Notes for Activity 49

STEP-BY-STEP PROCEDURE

Step 1: Introduce the subject of employee recognition:

"Think of the last time you worked for someone or were part of a team when you believe you were very motivated. How did you feel? What kind of results did you achieve? How did the manager or team leader treat you?"

Ask participants if they know what motivates people to work. Tell them that this is the focus of the next exercise.

Divide the group into pairs and ask each pair to arrange their chairs so they are facing one another. Distribute Handout 49.1, *Role Play Cards*. Ask one person to play the role of leader and the second to play the role of employee. They should act out role plays #1 and #2.

Role Play #1: Ask the "manager" to read the card and then start the role play.

Manager: Tell your employee that you received the final report on his team's project. Say thanks, but go on to criticize how long he took. Point out various spelling errors in the report, tell him how you really wanted the formatting done, and so on.

Role Play #2: Ask the "manager" to read the card and then start the role play.

Manager: Tell your employee that you received the final report on the team project. Thank him or her and hand the employee an invitation to a celebration.

Step 2: Discuss the two role plays.

Ask employees in the first role play how it felt in the second role play. (Have them try to stay in character when they explain.)

Ask managers what kind of results you are likely to get with the first method. What about the second?

Then ask everyone: How can we recognize employees for their work, yet still give the necessary criticism constructively?"

Discuss participants' ideas on this question. Then ask, "Which works best? To ignore? To give negative feedback? Or to give positive feedback?"

Someone will invariably point out that the opposite of love is not hate—it is to be ignored. So, the worst thing to do is to ignore the person's effort or accomplishment. Being negative is the next worst.

Step 3: Positive feedback works best, yet it is the least used. Cite the following and write it on a flipchart, if possible, so people can copy it down:

➔ What do employees want from their employer or leader?

58%–To use my time wisely
52%–To have a well-managed company
50%–To use my talents sensibly
41%–To assign me only clearly defined tasks
39%–To provide experiences that will enhance my career
31%–To thank me!

Distribute Handout 49.2, *Keep the Flame Burning–Recognizing Others*, then continue your presentation by pointing out these interesting facts (first quiz the group on what they think):

➔ The number one reason why people leave their positions is lack of praise.

➔ In one study, managers listed "money and job security" as the top motivator they thought employees would want. What did employees list? Full appreciation for a job well done!

➔ Employees want open communication, and they want to be treated with a sense of respect and trust. Leaders must encourage feedback and suggestions, and they must pay attention to them.

➔ In one study of 1,500 people:

58% seldom, if ever, received personal thanks.
76% seldom, if ever, received written thanks.
81% seldom, if ever, received public praise.

➔ Important principles:

1. Top-motivating incentives must be initiated by the leaders themselves, and they must be based on performance.

2. Recognition must take place as soon as possible after the achievement.

3. Recognition must happen frequently. As Ken Blanchard says, *Catch people doing things right!*

Step 4: Now it's time to practice giving positive feedback. Explain the four parts of positive feedback with this example:

I saw what you did.
I appreciate it.
Here's why it is important.
Here's how it made me feel.

Ask each pair to think of two people who deserve positive recognition. Ask them to apply the formula just outlined and practice giving recognition out loud with their partner.

Back in the total group, discuss how well this formula worked. Discuss their responses and ask for suggestions as to how people can use this method at work and at home.

Step 5: Close the session by lighting a candle and enthusiastically remind people to *keep the flame of enthusiasm and achievement burning* by positively recognizing their employees.

POST-ACTIVITY REVIEW

Take time shortly after conducting this activity to reflect on how it went, how engaged the participants were, and what questions they raised. Then, make notes that include how much time you actually spent on the activity.

Role Play Cards

Role Play #1

Manager: Tell your 'employee' you received the final report on his team's project, says thanks, but go on to criticize how long they took, point out spelling errors in the report, tell him how you really wanted the formatting done, etc.

Role Play #2

Manager: Tell your 'employee' you received the final report on his team's project, says thanks, and hand over an invitation to a celebration.

Keep the Flame Burning– Recognizing Others

What motivates you to work?

Research studies have revealed important information about employee motivation.

Important Statistics:

In one study, respondents revealed what they want most from their employers:

58%–To use my time wisely
52%–To have a well-managed company
50%–To use my talents sensibly
41%–To assign me only clearly defined tasks
39%–To provide experiences that will enhance my career
31%–To thank me!

In one study of 1,500 people:

58% of the respondents said that they seldom, if ever, receive personal thanks.
76% of the respondents said that they seldom, if ever, receive written thanks.
81% of the respondents said that they seldom, if ever, receive public praise.

Important principles:

1. At a minimum, employees want praise and a thank you!
2. Top-motivating incentives must be suggested and put in place by the leaders of the organization, and they must be based on performance.
3. Recognition must take place soon after the achievement or action warranting the reward.
4. Recognition must take place frequently. Catch people doing things right!

KEEP THE FLAME BURNING—RECOGNIZING OTHERS (continued)

Practice giving positive feedback!

I saw what you did.
I appreciate it.
Here's why it is important.
Here's how it made me feel.

Ten Ways to Motivate Your Employees

1. Create an environment that is open, encouraging, and fun.

2. Involve your employees in tasks that fit their experience and interests.

3. Respect their busy lives. Find out what they can manage to fit in, and be flexible.

4. Give them work to do in small chunks and tasks that they can complete in a timely fashion.

5. Provide employees with clear instructions, a manual, and other pertinent information.

6. Involve employees in decision-making.

7. Provide timely and specific feedback.

8. Give them your personal thanks, and do it often.

9. Plan recognition and rewards that fit the individual.

10. Celebrate their accomplishments!

50

ADD HEART TO YOUR WORKPLACE

Celebrations

Overview of Activity

Celebrations are becoming more frequent in the workplace. They are energizing, motivating, and supportive ways to empower employees. This module offers many ideas for celebrations. When teams work together for long periods of time, they should be encouraged to take frequent energy breaks to keep their ideas flowing. This exercise will help, as will its practical tips on snacks, water, and physical activity.

Objectives

→ To identify what kinds of celebrations participants have held or seen in the workplace.

→ To present the HEART formula.

→ To create a plan to incorporate more celebrations into the workday.

Setting Up the Activity

GROUP SIZE
Up to 20 participants

ESTIMATED TIME
1 hour

TRAINING METHODS
→ Presentation
→ Personal reflection
→ Group discussion

MATERIALS
Handout 50.1: *The HEART Formula*

EQUIPMENT AND SUPPLIES
→ Balloons
→ Streamers
→ Napkins with hearts on them
→ Banners that say *Congratulations! Let's Celebrate!*
→ Different hats (one for each participant)
→ Cloak and wand for the facilitator
→ Batons
→ Candles (for the cake)
→ Food and beverages
→ Basket for cards
→ Music

ROOM SET-UP
Using many of the supplies listed above, decorate the meeting room to look like a celebration. Chairs arranged in a semicircle.

Comments

Many leaders will provide appropriate recognition to their employees and team members but few remember to hold celebrations. Authors like Kouzes and Posner plus Deal and Key have done excellent research on the benefits of celebrations and provide numerous suggestions. This module will help leaders plan meaningful celebrations at work!

RESOURCES
Encouraging the Heart by James Kouzes and Barry Posner (San Francisco: Jossey-Bass) 2003.
Corporate Celebration: Play, Purpose, and Profit at Work by Terrence E. Deal and M.K. Key (San Francisco: Berrett-Koehler Publishers, Inc.) 1998.
The H.E.A.R.T. formula was created by Ken Blanchard, Lois Hart and Mario Tomayo and is included here with their permission.

VARIATIONS

Form small groups of 5 to 7 people each. Give each group a different case study that exemplifies various reasons to hold a celebration. Examples include:

→ The organization has recently clarified its vision and mission.

→ The company met the challenge of reversing 9/11's impact on sales.

→ The project team has reached the midpoint for completion of its year-long research effort.

Provide props, products, CDs, and art materials for the groups to use. Each group must make a large poster-size invitation to their celebration, and should select one piece of appropriate music to the season for the celebration.

Give the groups 20 minutes to plan.

Each group should describe its plan. Ask all the groups (after all have presented) to talk about the best thing each group did in their plan. Then everyone can vote on which group best represented the "HEART" formula. The prize is a large heart—perhaps a heart box of chocolates to share.

Trainer's Notes for Activity 50

STEP-BY-STEP PROCEDURE

Step 1: Outside the training room (which has been decorated), ask each person to fill out a card telling about a celebration they attended at work that was meaningful to them. Instruct them to drop their cards into a large basket at the door. They should then select a hat to wear.

Open the door with great fanfare (tooting a horn, for example). They will be entering a decorated room filled with the music of celebration.

Step 2: After participants settle in and are enjoying the treats you have provided, bring the basket with their cards to the front of the room. Pull out the examples, one at a time, and ask each contributor to talk about the celebration they referred to on their card. Take notes on the flipchart of the elements found in these celebrations.

Step 3: Then ask, "What are the ingredients of a wonderful Celebration?"

Present the HEART formula. (Distribute Handout 50.1, *The HEART Formula.*)

Ask them who plans the celebration. "It starts with *you,* the leader."

Reaffirm how important it is for the leader to get the ball rolling in planning a celebration. People need to know, up front, that the leader believes there is something worth celebrating.

Review who else might be involved. Outline these roles:

1. The Celebration Team: Create a small group of people who can help plan celebrations. Membership in this team should rotate periodically.

2. The Event Planner: Include the company planner, but don't make him or her totally responsible.

3. The Project or Team Leader: This person needs to plan how and why to celebrate at various points in the project's "life," as well as at the completion of the project. Milestones are important times.

Step 4: Pose the following questions for discussion:

What have you learned about celebrations?
What is your plan of action?
Now GET READY TO CELEBRATE!

POST-ACTIVITY REVIEW

Take time shortly after conducting this activity to reflect on how it went, how engaged the participants were, and what questions they raised. Then, make notes that include how much time you actually spent on the activity.

The HEART Formula

Celebrations must have H E A R T. They should be:

♥ **H**eartfelt

Celebrations should reflect your vision, mission, and values.

Celebrations must be initiated by the leaders of the organization, and must be based on performance and the organization's goals.

Celebrations are heartfelt.

The leader is the head of the celebration.

Celebrations are human events.

♥ **E**nthusiastic

Celebrations are fun, happy, and memorable.

Suggest and use different kinds of music for each celebration.

Show products and props.

♥ **A**ll-Inclusive

Invite customers or spouses to the celebration.

Thank them publicly for their part in the achievement.

♥ **R**ecognition

Celebrations recognize work outcomes and people.

They renew the spirit.

Be sure you make recognition part of the celebration.

♥ **T**imely

Celebrations must happen frequently.

Catch people doing things right!

Celebrations must occur around the time of the achievement or event that deserves or needs to be recognized (as soon as possible)

The H.E.A.R.T. formula was created by Ken Blanchard, Lois Hart and Mario Tomayo and included here with their permission.

GLOSSARY OF TRAINING METHODS*

ANALOGY: Two items that are similar or comparable in certain respects.

APPLICATION: Instructions or an assignment that puts the new learning into practice or use.

ASSESSMENT: The student reflects or uses an instrument to evaluate her/his strengths, values, position on issues, or developmental needs.

CARD SORT: Multiple items or ideas are listed on separate pieces of paper or cards; participants sort, group or rank them.

CASE STUDY: A printed description of a realistic problem or scenario that provides sufficient detail for participants to determine appropriate actions.

COACHING: A one-to-one real-time dynamic when an objective person (either the trainer or participant) listens and asks questions, while the second person poses a problem she/he wants to resolve.

DEMONSTRATION: The trainer (or a participant) shows how something works or can be used by "walking" participants through each step.

DISCUSSION: The trainer encourages dialogue among the participants (either in the total group or in small groups) about an issue or content from the workshop, using preplanned and spontaneous questions.

FEEDBACK: Use of a process (either verbal or as instrument) that provides information back to the individual.

JOURNALING: Written record of thoughts, reactions, or feelings.

METAPHOR: A word or phrase ordinarily and primarily used for one thing or purpose is applied to an explanation of another.

MOVEMENT: Activity that involves walking, milling about, and/or stretching, sometimes to music.

PRESENTATION: A planned talk, sometimes called a *lecturette*, to inform, report, instruct, motivate, or persuade.

REFLECTION: A quiet activity in which one writes or thinks about an issue or content from the workshop.

ROLE PLAY: Enactment of a real-life incident or event, or a created dramatized story that gives participants the opportunity to practice and experiment with new behaviors, and then receive feedback.

ROUND ROBIN: When, in an orderly fashion, participants verbally and in turn complete sentence stems or make remarks.

SENTENCE STEMS: The beginning of a sentence is provided, generally by the trainer, and the participant fills out the rest of the sentence with his/her own observation.

SIMULATION: An activity that gives the appearance of a real-life situation or experience.

STORYTELLING: Telling of a happening or connected series of happenings, whether true or fictional.

SYMBOL: Something that stands for, represents, or suggests another thing.

TACTILE: Touching or handling of objects.

VIDEO: Visual form of a movie, pre-taped.

VISUALIZATION: Formation of a mental visual image; once developed, it is often shared verbally or in writing.

WRITING: Putting thoughts, reactions, and feelings to paper or in electronic form.

---

*Hart, Lois B. *Training Methods That Work,* Los Altos: Crisp Publications, 1991.

INDEX